CRIME IN COLONIAL NEW ORLEANS

TERROR ON THE FRONTIER

DAVID MICHAEL SCHNEIDER

THE History PRESS

Published by The History Press
An imprint of Arcadia Publishing
Charleston, SC
www.historypress.com

First published 2025

Manufactured in the United States

ISBN 9781467159159

Library of Congress Control Number: 2025940397

This book is dedicated to my mother, my grandmother,
my grandfather, my sister and my chosen family, one and all.
We are the small histories that make a big difference.

CONTENTS

ACKNOWLEDGEMENTS

This work would not be possible without a constellation of people and resources doing the hard work of preserving Louisiana history for the last 150 years. Local historical societies and state-level initiatives have made this work possible. Members of the Louisiana Historical Society's greatest generation, those who translated and catalogued a huge portion of the notarial records in the early part of the twentieth century, are the single greatest contributors to this work. Without their scribbled notes, typewriter sheets and mind-boggling ability to determine what curve is which letter, many of the stories contained in this book would still be completely obscured. Unfortunately, many of these historians are nameless contributors. Their contributions have been relegated to comically dusty tomes. But their work floated down the course of time and into the hands of an over-tired, coffee-stained high school teacher—as well as other, far more competent researchers—and we are all the better for their effort. The current generation of historians and archivists who work at Tulane University, the New Orleans Jazz Museum and the Louisiana Historical Center have all dedicated themselves to an essential profession. I hope that this book serves to instill a degree of respect for those who selflessly toil to preserve the past for public benefit.

I owe a debt to the Landrieu family for their support throughout the whole process. Without them, this work would not be possible. I would also like to thank my place of work and the students who suffered under me while I composed this manuscript. If any of you students happen to be reading this right now, you are the reason that I worked so hard to finish this book. I believe this book contributes to making a better world for all of us. Remember that history and education need to have a purpose.

INTRODUCTION

The frontiers of civilization and its crimes are wedded to one another. From the most common burglaries to the desperate attempts at freedom by runaway slaves, be it the honorable duels among young gentlemen or the fights to the death on the edges of the world, crime defined the boundaries of colonial life. The frontier exists between the untamed wilds and the institutions of order so firmly rooted within a kingdom, country or empire. And so far away from civilization, the empire is different. The rules of life break down. Basic needs—bread, soap, water, care for the newborn and the sick—necessities that are well-provided for in the core of a sufficient civilization are scarce on the frontier. Suddenly, resources need to be renegotiated. But the courts, the churches and the king's law are at their most distant, most antiquated and most irrelevant. In these conditions, frontier crime rises from the depths of human capability.

Empathy and good sense demand that we understand why this is the case. Why would men fight and kill each other over forty paper notes belonging to a kingdom half a world away? Why would a slave seek to poison his master if he knew the consequences included an unconscionably horrible death? And why would a man feel the need to own slaves when the social and political system around him is already designed to make everyone else subservient? Being appointed governor of some far-away land that less than one thousand Europeans have ever seen, what would drive one to rob the colony blind, to attack the nearby nations, to spread corruption and deny services to those who needed it most? Plumbing the crimes that occur on the frontier, the edge of society, allows us to sense the depths of how empires treated their citizen-settlers.

This is no less the case in New Orleans, a city known for its criminal heritage. The placement of the city born in sin in the heart of the swampy Mississippi lowlands and the city's reputation for crime are not coincidental. In the first decade of settlement, crime in colonial Louisiana rose out of the needs of the settlers not being met by the French colonial system that deposited them at the edge of the known world. These colonists were a motley crew that had been deported to the colony as often as having willingly decided to go, especially if one considers the enslaved Africans in their number. The initial settlers were as unprepared to handle the Louisiana wildlands as the succession of governors that attempted to ground the project in profit for the colonial French empire. And the profitability of French Louisiana was an economic necessity that transcended all other concerns for its leaders. The materials that people most needed—linen, ships, wood, land, sundries and cattle—were the very things that nobody could afford to import. A colonial government composed of only a few dozen people at most had no ability to account for its needy citizens. The care of the needy tended to fall to the Catholic religious orders. However, these orders had never carried much truck in New France. And thus, much of the crime in colonial Louisiana centered on these unmet needs. Colonial Louisiana's legal enforcement was dominated by the need for materials to be secure, rather than the needs of people. This unstable colonial society in the first decade of settlement was disordered by individuals struggling to provide for themselves in a new environment and the impossibility of managing the colony effectively by the early French settlers in the conditions they found themselves in.

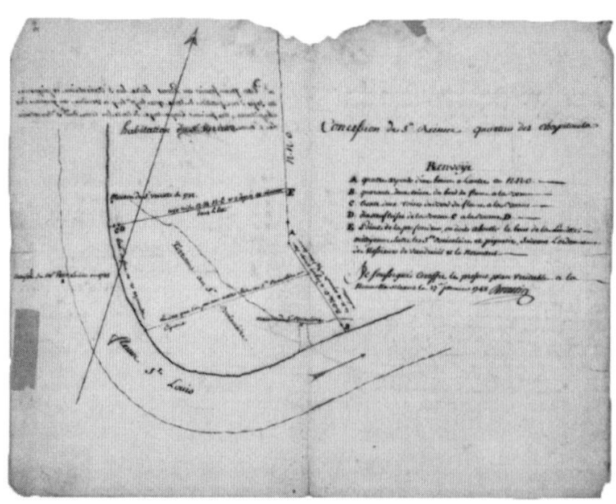

A snapshot of the simple beauty found in the colonial archives. This is a small legal map of a concession that was in dispute around January 1748. *Provided by the Louisiana Colonial Document Digitization Project, # 1748-01-27-03 (01).*

Colonial Louisiana, at its height, stretched north to south from the frosty sea edges of New Foundland to where the Mississippi River meets the Gulf of Mexico and east to west from the tip of Idaho to the edge of Kentucky. For eighty years, from when de la Salle planted his cross at the mouth of the Mississippi River to the embarrassment of the Seven Years' War, the entire heartland of the North American continent labored under the dominion of the distant French kings couched and lounging in their palace at Versailles. From the beginning, the venture's stated aim was profit for the kingdom. Because of this, the French administrators never felt the need to establish much more than fur trading outposts, forts and the bare necessities for a port town here and there. Inside of this region, uncounted Native American nations, rough and tough colonial fur traders, adventurers seeking gold and silver, imported settlers to a strange land and representatives of the king formed a murky, interwoven network that both mimicked and defied traditional French society. The region of New France sported a variety of extreme climates. Frozen, harsh, dense Canadian forests turned south and became the endless plains of the Midwest, complete with the godlike power of tornadoes and blizzards, scorching summers, freezing winters and scores of potentially hostile Native American nations that had no use for French traders. Coming down the Mississippi, the land turns from flat to hilly as one crosses from the plains into the American Southeast. The forests grow dense again. The land slopes ever downward. The heat and the humidity combine. The mosquitoes, gnats and horseflies harry travelers and spread disease. And then, finally, one comes to the mouth of the Mississippi and the miles of impenetrable semisoft, waterlogged swamps that would become known as the Gulf South. It was, in a word, a terrifying prospect to try to traverse such an unyielding strip of the continent. Attempting to settle it must have seemed an impossible and tantalizing task.

Despite being claimed by de la Salle at the mouth of the Mississippi River, today's Louisiana Gulf Coast, the colony's government was diffuse. Its center varied between modern-day Mississippi, Alabama, Louisiana and Quebec. Different governors represented the king in various subdivisions, and what centralization could be done was often done in Paris. In the Canadian territories, rough Frenchmen risked life for the liberties afforded to those who could collect pelts by hunting wildlife or trading with the First Nations. The French saw profit in pelts, so the royal attention was directed there. Following the money, the first French settlers came to St. Lawrence River in Canada, not the Gulf South, seeking freedom and a living. But over time, as the French began to realize the scale of their acquisition by claiming the entire Mississippi River basin as their own, royal interest began to shift southward. Further acquisitions in the Caribbean in 1635 opened up the opportunity to become gloriously wealthy exporting cash crops. The French colony of Haiti became profitable, and it needed to be protected from the Spanish, the English and the privateers and pirates. The French kingdom needed to control trade up the Mississippi as well, since the English colonies were steadily growing toward the Appalachian Mountains and becoming hungrier for westward land as the generations passed. The small Gulf South colony of Mobile could not suit the purpose. For one, situated at the mouth of the Mobile River, it was neither ideal for trade nor turning a profit that suited the kingdom's mounting debts. In 1702, Jean-Baptiste Le Moyne de Bienville founded the colony of Mobile, nothing more than a fort and a deepwater port on a nearby island, as an initial foothold in the region. It had never grown to much more than a couple hundred people, and the Mobile River and Mobile Bay did not provide the access to the Mississippi that heavy eighteenth-century trading vessels needed.

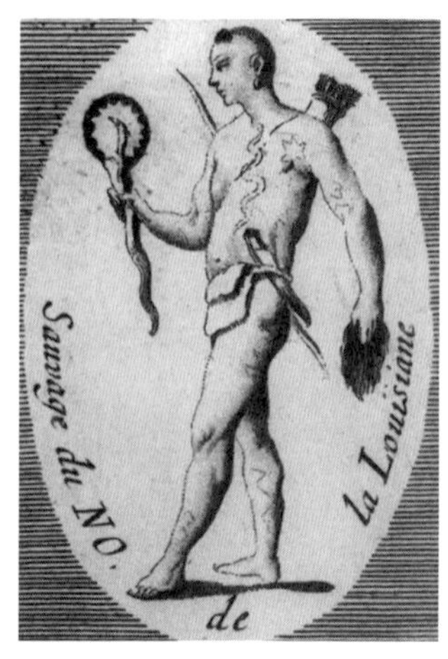

An eighteenth-century drawing of a Native American warrior. The warrior is depicted holding a scalp and a snake. The French had a long history of warfare and diplomacy with the Southeast tribes. *Retrieved from the Library of Congress Digital Collection, img1.png (25).*

Bienville chose the spot for Mobile with his brother Pierre Le Moyne d'Iberville, but he chose the spot for New Orleans on his own. In 1717, Bienville began exploring westward, looking for a port that would be defensible from raiders and protected from the choppy waters where the Mississippi meets the Gulf. Sailing up the river, Bienville found a crescent-shaped island adjacent to the Mississippi and surrounded by dense swamp. The Native American population did not have many, if any, permanent settlements in the area. But the explorers soon learned that the Native Americans used this area for hunting, fishing and as a quick throughway between Lake Pontchartrain and the Mississippi River. When Bienville and the settlers disembarked, the Isle d'Orleans could have only been what it was: a muddy, swampy throughway, laden with wildlife, deep brush and a hostile climate. A few rogue settlers scattered along Bayou Saint John offered some familiarity to Bienville and his men—but the presence of a complex network

This is a piece from Paris in 1758 depicting the hunting practices of the Native Americans. The French were interested in Native hunting practices as a part of the lucrative fur trade. *Retrieved from the Library of Congress Digital Collection, img4.jpg (28).*

of migrating, hunting and gathering Native peoples must have been daunting. Still, Bienville saw promise where no one else did. And in 1718, he founded the colony of New Orleans with the blessing of his French imperial administrators. The purpose? Profit and glory.

The point of this book is twofold. The first is to give voice to people from the period following the founding of New Orleans. In and of itself, this is a worthy goal. The characters from this past world speak clear and true today to our needs and concerns. The plots of women like Anne Mony, to steal a French ship and sail to the English colonies, rings true in the hearts of every person who seeks to be free. But it also rhymes across time with the epidemic of car-jackings that has caught local attention in the last few years. The car thieves tend to be young, poor and seeking something that their world cannot provide for them. So too with Anne Mony. And though it may be macabre, men like Pontuel and Laborde, fishermen fighting over a handful money, give some sense of connection to the petty offenses that devolve into violent crimes today. For modern New Orleanians, the connection to these figures long-gone should be visceral. The pathway between Lake Pontchartrain and the river that caught Bienville's eye is likely still traveled today, whether it be Wisner, Old Gentilly Road or Elysian Fields. This means that human beings have been commuting from the lake to the river and back since the misty dawn of Native American civilization in the area. That same commute attracted European settlement to the region. Our roots go deeper into the soil than we realize. And like all good history, these stories and revelations seek to entertain the reader as well.

The second point of this book is to provide an explanation for the broad trend of lawbreaking that defined the Basse-Louisiane, or "lower Louisiana," in a way that reaches from history into the present. In this, the book will consistently highlight two key features of French Louisiana settlement and argue that they gave rise to the lawbreaking sinner's society that defines New Orleans to this day. The first is the climate itself. It turns out that Bienville's appraisal of the Isle d'Orleans was not universal. Other explorers thought that Bienville made an error in establishing the colony where it is, and for good reason. For one, it is too far away from Haiti to provide the more profitable sister colony very much protection, let alone Biloxi or Mobile. For another, the ground is inundated with water, all buildings and roads sink into the mud inevitably and Bienville got it all wrong by thinking New Orleans would be more protected from hurricanes than other ports along the Gulf Coast. The summers in New Orleans outdid the summers almost anywhere else, especially in Illinois territory and French Canada, and while the winters were mild, they were also wet and no sure reprieve from heat, bugs or disease. The Isle d'Orleans rested far afield of the rest of the French holdings in the West Indies and Gulf South and could not be adequately supplied. Compounded with the French policy that colonies should rely on the mother country for most manufactured goods, that old bane of the free market known as mercantilism, this meant that New Orleans rarely had enough necessary supplies for everyone. And this touches on the second cause of lawbreaking and criminality in Basse-Louisiane: the administrators operating in these conditions were under no strong obligation to provide for the needs of their subjects. The realities of colonial administration made this impossible and undesirable. New France, the entire French colonial system from Canada to the Gulf, was divided into administrative regions. Even among these divided regions, a colonial government might not consist of more than a handful of administrators at any given time. Especially in the early decades, the land-owning subjects were as much the hands of the king as the royal governor, in the sense that the only reason that the king's law prevailed at all was because of their shared need for some social bond.

One trend in the study of Louisiana is to blame some, if not all, of the criminality that springs forth in the Isle d'Orleans on the forced importation of convicts and prostitutes from France to the New World. However, this view does not do justice to the cause of Louisiana's ailments. When studying crime in colonial Louisiana, it is impossible to begin anywhere but with the arrival of the first laborers and soldiers to the region in the late seventeenth and early eighteenth centuries. From the beginning of French Louisiana, the dominant social tension had been between the social institution of the Catholic Church, which was responsible for the moral upkeep of ancien régime France, and the young men who were the initial fodder for development.[1] These young men came from diverse backgrounds within the French sphere of influence. Some of them were Canadian frontiersmen interested in making a living on the edge of society. Others were soldiers, young men from France who had few prospects at home and few prospects

This piece satirizes the practice of deporting prostitutes to Louisiana. French authorities hoped to spur the colony's growth by exporting women into Louisiana, especially those convicted of nuisance crimes like prostitution. *Retrieved from the Library of Congress Digital Collection, img3.jpg (27).*

in the colonies. Many were criminals. Many of the women were prostitutes. But even beyond the fallacious prejudgment of felons, soldiers and the lower class that underlies this argument, this explanation fails to characterize the actual causes of New Orleans' criminality. Frontier crime revolved around economic need caused by insufficient resources and a trying climate, especially in the first decades of colonial New Orleans' history. This dynamic is at its strongest beginning with the founding of New Orleans in 1718 and continuing to the conclusion of the Seven Years' War and the acquisition of the colony by Spain.

In this kind of history, we are not alone. The traditions of frontier history and frontier criminology help us establish the basic facts of life on the ground in colonial New Orleans. In the Louisiana territory, society broke down to a near unrecognizable point. Colonial economics and the fraying of social ties in new environments brought on intense social destabilization. In particular, marriage ties, the ties of subjects to king and the ties of fellow subjects with one another all dissolved on the frontier like salt dropped into water. Historians build these narratives by accessing public records, weaving together events in the colony and then drawing out the stories about individuals that speak to us across time.

This book builds on the social history of colonial Louisiana primarily by accessing archived court records relating to crime in New Orleans between 1718 and the 1760s. The French were studious in their attempts to build the king's power and solidify their own through effective use of the law. When it suited the purposes of those in charge, the law was a powerful tool. Precedence moved men in ways that were far more efficient than threatening every settler and slave with a gun. Colonial administrators were sure to keep what records they could. By examining the remaining records of these cases, this book shows that the first decades of colonial New Orleans' history was defined by a breakdown of social relations and crimes deriving from the unmet needs of the colonists. Of these hundreds of digitized documents and thousands more kept in libraries, the stories of a half-dozen French colonists during the period embody the struggle for survival and dignity experienced by the whole. Their stories are vastly different, and while their sufferings share characteristics, each is its own play worthy of a Grecian treatment. Hopefully, this book does them some small justice.

From a more academic perspective, existing literature on criminology and the social cohesion of the Louisiana colony shows that Louisiana struggled to maintain the social norms that existed in Europe. In "The Moral Climate of French Colonial Louisiana, 1699–1763," Brasseaux provides a plethora of examples illustrating how Louisiana's colonial culture differed significantly from the legal and social norms of France.[2] Jennifer Spear's "Colonial Intimacies: Legislating Sex in French Louisiana" explicitly links the introduction of colonial economics to the breakdown of social relations.[3] Multiple studies have explored how commodification broke down the social bonds of French society, most notably in the institution of marriage. French traders spread across the area and married into both Native and French societies in order to use either party to their advantage. These *coureurs de bois*, the wild fur traders of the French empire, acted as a nation unto themselves. This disrupted the traditional social bonds of both Native and European cultures.[4] The breakdown in social cohesion was also driven by the realities of high death rates in the colony's early years.[5]

Understanding the rarity of French women in the early decade of the New Orleans enterprise is key to understanding the prevalence and depth of resource scarcity in the colony. Women were disinclined to join the colonial

An early rendering of New Orleans, depicted as a small outpost upon the water. This small depiction of New Orleans has been cropped from a larger map that was produced by and for the Company of the West. *Retrieved from the Library of Congress Digital Collection.*

venture because of its perceived dangers, and thus there were less women in colonial Louisiana. The rarity of women was underscored by the dangers of childbirth in a settler setting and the relatively high mortality rate for colonists. An unprofitable French colony was unlikely to attract husbands and fathers with suitable daughters, and those daughters were unlikely to make more daughters; thus, New Orleans spent its first decade in a population spiral that early leaders like Bienville would attempt to solve. Sisyphus must have had a good laugh at Bienville's expense from down there in the Underworld. Ultimately, the introduction of education in the 1720s by the Ursuline Convent began to turn the tide toward stabilizing French colonial society's need for women as brides. At the same time, fur traders coming from Canada to the Isle d'Orleans introduced the practice of keeping Native American women as concubines, a form of sexual slavery that degraded women into commodities for European and Native American men to trade as resources. In New France, this practice was known as *métissage*. And while the early French administrators, and their Catholic Church counterparts, balked at the practice and pleaded with the colonists to stop, Sisyphus laughed at them, too. The frontiersmen would not give up their slaves or their most valuable commodities, and in New France, Native American women became both. In time, this system of Native American slavery would be replaced by a similar system of African slavery, which was closer to the more commonly understood aspects of American chattel slavery and continued to develop well into the eighteenth century, though this system did retain characteristics of sexual slavery.[6]

The peculiarities of European cultures led the stress of frontier life to present itself by heightening the social tension between colonists. For instance, in Spanish Florida, matters of honor and dishonor became an important part of managing the deep insecurities of colonial life. The Spanish courts had to expend time and resources managing the ill effects of rumors and slander. In an overburdened Spanish administration far from the homeland, it is notable that the powers-that-be would expend resources managing these affairs. And the consequences of rumors and slander could be dire to the reputation of society at large, too.[7] Louisiana was no slouch either and would in time become one of the dueling capitals in all of North America. In Louisiana, the particular lack of European women and the heightened sense of tension in settling a swampy woodland presented itself, in part, in the development of a form of sexual slavery, a large community of sex workers and an abundance of men willing to step outside of the boundaries set by the Catholic Church that governed French life at home.

Presented with these facts, any serious thinker must stop here and address what exactly is the nature of crime. The fundamental problem looks something like this: slavery is rightfully a crime today, but in the eighteenth century, it was not. And while in both the eighteenth century and the twenty-first century sex work is often criminalized, many today see it as an expression of bodily autonomy and thus no crime at all. And so, like an angry beast rising from the swampy deep, the question of state ethics rears its head. Questioning the ethics of each colonial law is well beyond the scope of this study. However, this research project draws from existing studies of colonial state-building. At the edge of the known world, *crime* is an ambivalent term at best.

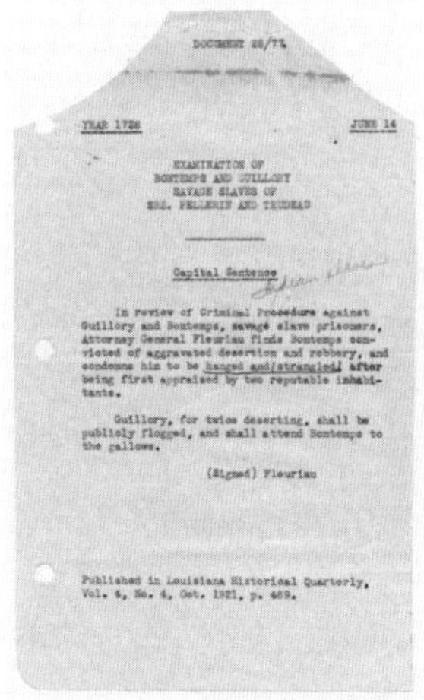

DOCUMENT 28/71

YEAR 1728 JUNE 14

EXAMINATION OF
BONTEMPS AND GUILLORY
SAVAGE SLAVES OF
SRS. PELLERIN AND TRUDEAU

Capital Sentence

In review of Criminal Procedure against Guillory and Bontemps, savage slave prisoners, Attorney General Fleuriau finds Bontemps convicted of aggravated desertion and robbery, and condemns him to be hanged and/strangled/ after being first appraised by two reputable inhabitants.

Guillory, for twice deserting, shall be publicly flogged, and shall attend Bontemps to the gallows.

(Signed) Fleuriau

Published in Louisiana Historical Quarterly, Vol. 4, No. 4, Oct. 1921, p. 469.

Bontemps and Guillory were both executed for running away from their masters. For the reader's benefit, they can read the summary of their sentencing document in English. Translated by the Louisiana Historical Society. *Provided by the Louisiana Colonial Document Digitization Project # 1728-06-14-03 (19).*

Following from the work of the broader colonial scholarship community, this book ventures to make a few assertions. Because colonial governments seek to provide for the needs of the colonial venture, the colonial government must constantly negotiate and renegotiate the rules of engagement within a context where resources are scarce, help is far away and danger seems omnipresent. And while criminal elements, those violating a law or social norm, are a core part of French Louisiana's early identity, scholars should not ignore the pervasive sense of state crime that governed the vast continental expanse as exemplified by the widespread reliance on penal colonists, the introduction of chattel slavery and specific events like the Natchez Massacre. In order to have any footing within this muddy waters, we must rely on bedrock claims. For the context here, the simple definition of a crime being a violation of a set law or norm is sufficient. However, these crimes arose out of the dire needs of colonists and the oppressive conditions within the colonies. And further, when these petty crimes are interrogated, they reveal the underlying conditions in French Louisiana that could be termed a *state crime* all in themselves. However, the book does not go so far as to declare the establishment of the colony itself a crime and does not posit that crime was the fundamental purpose of the French colonial project. French Louisiana was not a criminal enterprise, but it was inextricably tied to a criminal element that grew within it.

It is amazing how the few documents that we have from the French criminal courts in the early eighteenth century paint such vivid pictures of colonial life. Through hardly more than a handful of records in the colonial database, characters like Rivard du Vigne shine bright through the centuries. Though on the surface it appears that Rivard was a simple settler who inhabited the Gentilly area for a few decades in the early 1800s, a man who complained about Native American raiders, often served as a witness for document signing and once was sued over a road, within context this describes an exceptionally interesting life. Though the murder of Pontuel by Laborde seemed to take up very little space in the minds of French colonial officials, the details of the story offer fascinating insight into the dynamics between criminals foisted to the edge of the world to serve as colonial fodder and a single colonist who had enough honor to turn himself in. Even the events with a multiplicity of documents, like the plotted theft of a French vessel from the Port of Orleans, come through with clarity, drama and intrigue.

Below all of these stories are examples of needs being unmet and with little possibility of being met soon. Rivard's road was a key throughway, and its closure was a threat to colonial commerce and survivability. Pontuel and Laborde came to blows over the need for paper money, what could only have been a rare commodity for colonial fishermen. And whether it is nursing mothers sending their stepdaughters to steal linens, colonial men deciding that a slave is guilty of theft well before the law arrives or a dire plot by a baker and his wife to steal a vessel and sail to the English colonies, the stories of crime in French Louisiana are all underpinned by the pressing needs of its inhabitants pushed to extremes to survive and a colonial government unequipped to assess and provide for its subjects.

Works like "The Moral Climate of French Colonial Louisiana, 1699–1763,"[8] "Slanders and Sodomy: Studying the Past through Colonial Crime Investigation,"[9] "American Indians in Colonial New Orleans"[10] and "Plotting the Natchez Massacre: Le Page Du Pratz, Dumont de Montigny, Chateaubriand" provide context that allows us to understand the shifting investigators, rough-and-tumblers and those just barely getting by, as well as the larger events that shaped the character of French Louisiana and its inhabitants.[11] This body of work provides additional context to the research and allows this project to focus primarily on the minutiae of French colonial crime and what it illuminates about the day-to-day life of French colonists in French Louisiana, especially the New Orleans and Gulf Coast regions.

The legacy of French colonization on crime and justice today is tangible. One need only look at the French brand of justice. Represented in paintings like *Branded With Fleur De Lis A Symbolic Link to Slavery—The Code Noir or the Black Code*, communities in Louisiana still have a visceral closeness to the effects of colonization.[12] Uncovering the past pain that occurred at the very foundations of the city also reveals the fundamental characteristics, material, social and political, that bind us together and, optimistically, provide sites for concentrated improvement today.

1

PETTY AND HIGH CRIMES IN NEW FRANCE

On a cool midsummer day in August 1717,[13] a royal proclamation from the court of King Louis XV declared that all drafts of notarized documents in the Louisiana territory must be preserved. The young king probably had very little to do with the proclamation in his name. In 1717, Louis XV had been ruling for a mere two years and was only seven years old. On that day in August, the weather in the two locations could not have been more different. Versailles had been the natural habitat of the Bourbon kings since Louis XIV built the monument to his own majesty in 1631. The Versailles region is a temperate, woody, green hill scape with summer temperatures that rarely rise above the mid-seventies. And beyond that, the land had long ago been domesticated as the Sun King sought to domesticate France's nobility. The Sun King's endless wars, first with the Dutch and then with the Spanish and finally all of Europe, had drained the royal treasury, but Versailles' majesty was still unparalleled a generation later. On that day, there is no doubt that Louis XV rose in the morning, had attendants dress him and slip his slippers on while royal ministers bowed and begged entrance and may have even enjoyed a nice epicurean salad or a cup of hot chocolate.[14]

At the same time, across the Atlantic and the Gulf of Mexico, the sun set on the undeveloped Isle d'Orleans. In a little less than a year, Jean Baptiste de Moyne, Sieur de Bienville, would sail across the swampy island and launch a project of permanent settlement that would result in the city of New Orleans. But for now, on a humid August night in 1717, only local

Louis XV was fond of the luxurious aspects of life at Versailles. Beyond a love of hot chocolate, a rare treat derived from New World plants, Louis XV reportedly loved to see himself in sculpture. Of course, even the wealthy in Louisiana could afford no such thing during their time in the colony. *Image provided by the Metropolitan Museum, as a gift of George Blumenthal, 1941.*

Native tribes and scattered European settlers inhabited the island, and only temporarily. The Native tribes crossed through the swamps along a single overland route that connected the Mississippi River and Lake Pontchartrain. The route was short enough and dry enough that one could carry their canoe on their backs and make the jaunt between important waterways. The French would come to call these ancient walking paths the *portages*. Walking overland, one traded alligators hidden in the dark waters for swamp cats prowling the tree line. Anyone traveling the old path would have welcomed the arrival of the broad Pontchartrain or swirling Mississippi waters by the end. The air was thick, hot and full of mosquitoes, and one had to travel in order to cool off. A few European settlers had come to the area along Bayou St. Jean from Mobile in 1708, and now even fewer were left. Wheat would not grow here, so what use was the land? That night, Native Americans and European settlers used the Isle d'Orleans in the same way that it had been used for a millennia—a hot, muggy place to travel through and rarely, if ever, a place to stay.

The corporate enterprise that managed the vast Louisiana territory had a shifting set of names that changed to suit its purposes. Today, it is more commonly referred to with the name it was given at birth, the

Mississippi Company. In 1717, as the king, or really the king's regents, were declaring notarized documents sacrosanct, an enterprising young Scotsman named John Law bought the company, and he would change the name according to the needs of the courtiers in Versailles and his own banking schemes. Though it is counterintuitive, the removal of the Louisiana territory from the bosom-ownership of the king and delegation to the company's men—and of all men a foreigner—was an act meant to increase the power, wealth and prestige of the French kingdom within the Louisiana territory, not lessen it. The Kingdom of France was deeply in debt. The Louisiana territory was the largest undeveloped tract of land with any economic potential in the French empire. And it seems that the sunny, temperate courtiers of Versailles decided it was time to get serious about the Louisiana territory.

The colonial records related to the New Orleans region of French Louisiana began documenting petty crimes around 1723. By that point, the colony was settled enough that the enforcement of property rights and the administration of the king's justice could begin in earnest. In 1719, a royal decree established judges to oversee the colony, but that does not mean that social cohesion was achieved. Far from it. And even as petty crimes began to unfold, far more serious crimes were the first tasks the colonial administration had to contend with. The crimes of the 1720s revolved around two determining factors that would set the pattern for Louisiana's colonial crime in general. The first factor was geography. Based on the surviving documents from French courts, colonial authorities seem to have been keen on bringing the justice of courts to the Port of Orleans, the fishing regions between Orleans and Biloxi and the outlying swampy areas that French colonists settled that are today known as Gentilly and Jefferson Parish. These areas were likely hotbeds for crimes like burglary, theft and murder, and at the very least the crimes that the colonial authorities could remand during the decade of the 1720s tend to revolve around those areas. Bringing the king's law much farther north was unthinkable in the initial decades of settlement. Illinois country was supposed to be a land of silver, not a land of laws. Neither would manifest under French rule.

The second factor that determined the nature of crimes was the lack of essential goods. Surviving texts from the era, like the diary of Francois-Xavier de Charlevoix, paint the region of Basse-Louisiane as one of desperate need. The diary of François-Xavier de Charlevoix provides a firsthand account of New Orleans in 1722. The diary entries show that the city of New Orleans had developed some renown within francophone

North America. But when de Charlevoix finally arrived in New Orleans, he gave the colony a lukewarm review. He questioned Bienville's arguments about the colony's superior placement, worried about the ability of the colony to respond to other parts of the Gulf Coast in case of crisis, and commented that the people of New Orleans were camped on the banks of the Mississippi waiting for plans to arrive that would "ne sera pas aussi aisé de l'exécuter, qu'il l'a été de le tracer sur le papier" (not be as easy to execute as they were to draw on paper, essentially, "Easier said than done"). De Charlevoix's skeptical view of New Orleans reveals the limits of colonial rule and the anxieties of the French ruling class concerning the colony. The French ruling class was worried about invasion, the speed of boats, relations with the Native Americans and the security of concessions. They were not worried about the meager survival of menial subjects.

Marie Simon Lespronne and the Nature of Petty Crime

So it was that in the muggy spring months of 1723 a twelve-year-old named Marie Simon Lespronne was sent by her mother to collect linen from the estate of Chevalier de Morand, a landowner in the area. Marie was born in the Pays de Caux, Normandy, a cool-weather area along the coast of the English Channel. Caux is known for its gray chalk cliffs and cool valleys with plentiful running water. Though on the edges of the kingdom, the manorial system meant that Normandy's lords were close to their subjects and formed a complete, integrated community. No doubt, Marie had some recollection of her life in Normandy, the abundance of cool breezes and closeness of lords and priests with disposable wealth, as she trudged across brick and then mud and grass to the de Morand holding. Her stepmother, Marie Jans, could not get the linens herself. Madame Jans was engaged in wet nursing, a popular way to make money for women in France. It was expected that upper-class French women would be able to afford a wet nurse, and we can be sure that Marie Jans was nursing a child of some importance, either a local landowner or a royal official. Wet nursing offered a taste of the distant Parisian life for the landowners in Louisiana and a little extra money for Madame Jans. And in these early days of colonization, when life existed in "an unhealthy country, without bread without wine, without meat and without clothes,"[15] and births were rare and surviving infants rarer, this child was far too precious to leave alone to take outside for any length of time. Travel was certainly off the table, and so young Marie Laspronne would have to go collect the linens.

But linens were also rare, and the de Morands had no interest in giving up such precious resources. Luxury cost money, and while the land in the Mississippi Delta was fertile, all of the promises of silver flowing from mines in the interior of the continent down into the region had yet to manifest. Being landed in French Louisiana meant that you owned the roof over your head, enslaved the people who worked your estate and had the prestige that came with a sustainable income. In Louisiana, unlike in Europe, being landed did not mean decadence. In the colonies, luxuries came from closeness to the merchants and the royal administration, and even then those luxuries came at a hefty price. Without a doubt, in May 1723, when Marie Laspronne was sent to fetch linens from the de Morand estate, there was no intent on asking the family for a donation or a loan or bartering with them.

Many of the inhabitants of New Orleans suffered under the same wants as Marie Laspronne and Marie Jans. In the opening decade of the colony, these circumstances led to a rash of burglaries affecting some of the wealthier families in New Orleans and its outlying regions. The attorney general investigated each of these burglaries because the victims of these crimes were well-off property owners with some ties to the colonial regime. The details of these burglaries reveal evidence of a disordered society suffering under rigid hierarchies, a selective justice system and a dire lack of necessary supplies. And each of these crimes reveals interesting dynamics of which subjects found themselves pushed to the brink and who the French Crown was comfortable blaming and punishing.

In May 1723, Attorney General Fleuriau opened an investigation into the case of Marie Laspronne. Marie was interrogated on account of the missing linens from the de Morand residence. A peculiarity of French justice, or perhaps just the altered justice found in the colonies, was that interrogations were recorded only when it was time to sign a confession. We do not know who accused young Marie, but by the time she was taken into the city and confronted with a prosecutor, she was ready to talk. Again and again, the word that stands out among Marie's testimony is *aiguiller*, "to steer." In the official record, the young woman did not do this of her own accord. The trial began the next day and was adjourned on the grounds that Marie Jans was wet nursing at the time, but by that time the plot was fully unraveling. One of the women, likely young Marie Laspronne, implicated Marie Rousseau in the linen theft plot. Suddenly, the scandal touched multiple members of the ruling class. Marie Rousseau was married to Georges Ramond, a steward and planter for none other than Sieur de Bienville.

At this point, the case goes cold. Maybe because Madame Jans was wet nursing, or maybe because the situation suddenly had the potential to reflect poorly on the top echelons of colonial society, whatever further notarized records there were on this case appear to be lost. Many of these cases of petty theft and burglary were not resolved in recorded legal documents, or those records appear to have been lost. What we have left is the pattern of the French colonial regime—investigations were thorough, guilt was assigned implicitly, and the records almost uniformly failed to record the punishments carried out by the court. Cases were not resolved. They were accounted for. This speaks to the underlying premise of the colonial regime when Louis XV made his proclamation in August 1717. No matter what *les majesté* in Versailles thought, the majesty of the king did not hold the colonial project together. Only property rights could fulfill that function. Courts did not exist to mediate the law of the king. They existed to mediate the ownership of rare necessities.

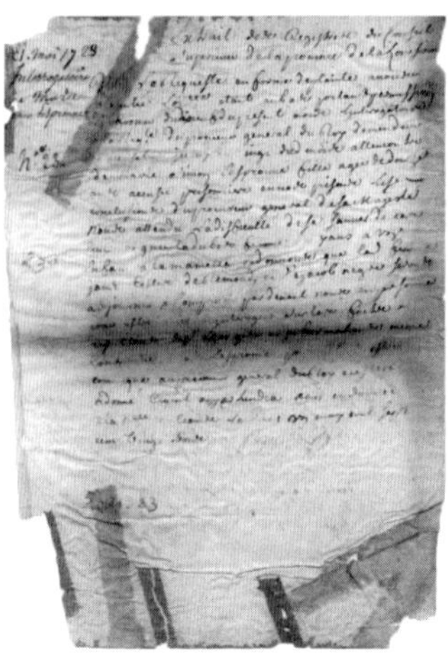

Marie Lespronne was subjected to the French interrogatory system. This means that she was confronted with her accusers until her story matched theirs or until the Superior Council was satisfied with her testimony. Proof of guilt or innocence comparable to modern standards of guilt was not required for rulings. *Provided by the Louisiana Colonial Document Digitization Project # 1723-05-21-01 (20).*

Burglaries on the Bayou: Property and Race

At the same time that the office of the attorney general was investigating the case of Marie Laspronne, troubling events on Bayou St. John demanded further attention from the regime. A handful of landowners and a boat captain reported catching a slave stealing goods from a lower-class white locksmith in the colony. This was no landed crime, and there are no primary sources that suggest why such a minor theft would merit the attention of the attorney general. However, by understanding the underlying nature of crime in colonial Louisiana—that the environment engendered crime and that crime arose from dire need—we can begin to fit the pieces into place. And there was a further complication, one that likely demanded the attention of the attorney general: the accused was an enslaved African.

The story of the settlers and the boat captain went that the locksmith, named Didier Gaspard in the notarized documents, was the victim of a nighttime burglary, and precious goods like linen, clothing and soap were taken from him. Whether or not the burglary had been reported to the colonial authorities, the crime garnered enough attention in the rumor mill that taskmaster and boat captain François Rilieux remembered the story after catching an enslaved man named Andre with a collection of basic goods. The items Andre was found with were described as "some articles of clothing, slippers, soap, etc."[16] And when Andre was found with these goods, goods that no chattel slave should have ever possessed in this abundance on their own, Rilieux ordered the man whipped until he confessed to the nature of his crime. Being whipped aboard a ship among the endless marshy lowlands and great expanse of Gulf waters could only have been traumatizing. It is unclear if Rilieux received a confession from Andre, but the story coalesced nonetheless. Rilieux made course for Gentilly with Andre and the goods in tow.

Of course, no records exist of Gaspard's robbery before May 22, and it is possible that the May 22 document arose out of Didier Gaspard reporting the robbery to the attorney general. If it had even been reported, there is little to suggest that the woes of a locksmith interested the attorney general before May 25, when a representative collected the stories of the witnesses. The colonial authorities were not in the business of chasing nameless, faceless burglars that had the good sense to prey on the lower classes. But they were in the business of keeping landowners like Rivard Du Vigne, François Dugay and Sieur Lagarde, who was Andre's owner, invested and happy with the colonial order. And the colonial authorities were certainly in the business of ensuring that naval order, commercial and military, and the hierarchy of chattel slavery remained stable and unchanged. So, Attorney General Fleuriau dispatched his man to investigate only after the other residents of Bayou St. John had involved themselves in the investigation, found someone to accuse and could now deliver the law to the Attorney General's Office to be stamped and waved away.

The scarcity of basic necessities is on clear display throughout the incident. That a burglary for basic items would have attracted the attention of the attorney general shows how valuable these items were. It also reveals how colonial subjects negotiated much of the legal process on their own. The law system of colonial France does not resemble the modern American system

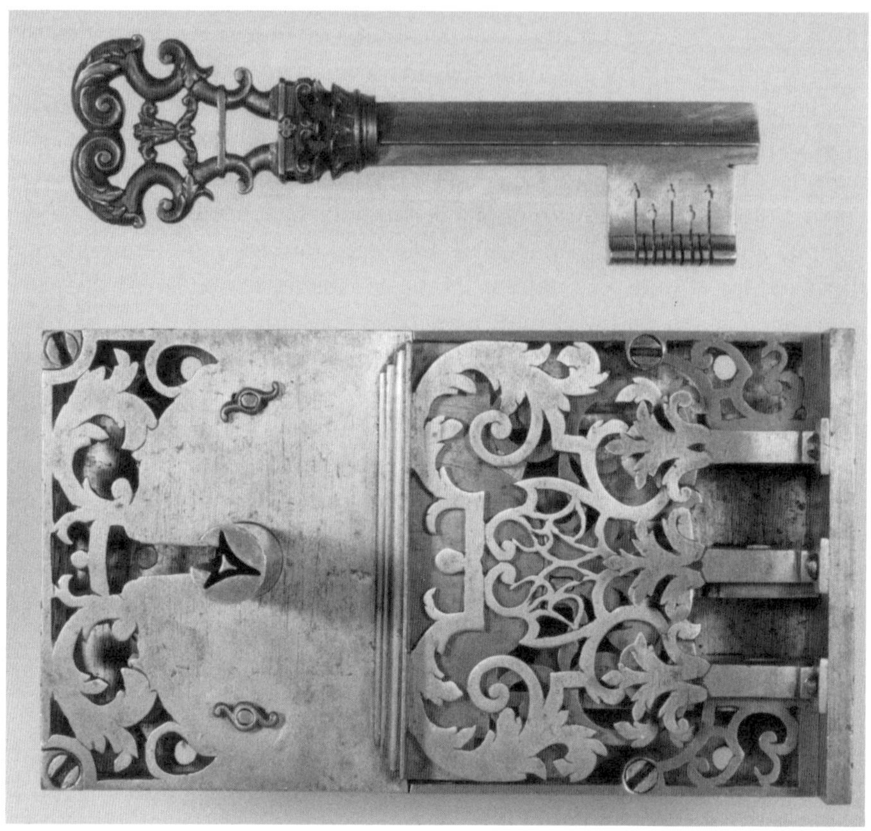

A typical example of the beautiful simplicity of eighteenth-century technology. This French lock predates the colonial Louisiana period by about twenty years. Men like Didier Gaspard made their living crafting exquisite and durable locks for their community. *Image provided by the Metropolitan Museum and the Harris Brisbane Dick Fund, 1957.*

in anything more than a passing glance. Before the investigator showed up, Andre was discovered, beaten and brought back to shore, and the stolen goods were returned to Gaspard. All that was left for the investigator was to catalogue the incident. The landowners resolved the dispute against the enslaved African in favor of a settler whose skills they likely needed. The order of the landowners having much, the settlers having some and the slaves having none was preserved. The Attorney General's Office accounted for the crime, and that was all. The case shows how in the absence of a strong legal presence, locals came together to resolve social transgressions and place blame where they thought it belonged, absent systems of justice. The burglary is blamed squarely on Andre, and there is no further record of attempts to discover any deeper truth to the matter. Again, the records do not include a formal legal resolution. But based on the climate of French Louisiana at the time—and the coming revisions to the Code Noir that would be written in part by powerful men like Bienville—it is likely that Andre was either beaten severely or executed.

The remaining recorded burglaries in 1723 reinforce the pattern of environmental factors leading to crimes that arose out of need for basic supplies. May, June and July are among the hottest months of the year. It is not surprising that the peak of the 1723 burglary wave crested in July with the theft of some silk stockings from a plantation owner named Joseph Chapron. Madame and Monsieur Le Roy were accused by Joseph Chapron of burglarizing his house in the city while he was away on his plantation overseeing his business affairs.[17] Again, Chapron was able to accuse the Le Roys because he had done the legwork of investigating by himself. According to Chapron, he tracked the theft to the Le Roys through two pairs of silk stockings that an associate of Chapron's arrived with in mid-July. This associate, Paul Barre, claimed an African woman sold them to him. The pair went to interrogate the woman, and they felt she had incriminated herself by changing her story and presenting Chapron with the second set of silk stockings. She turned the stockings over to Chapron, and after filing the initial report on July 13, 1723, he presented his accusation again to the court the next day. All of the witnesses gave their testimony by the fifteenth.

The case of the Le Roys follows our established pattern: civil investigation, criminal accusations and no records of resolution. But there are some twists to this case worth interrogating further. Monsieur Le Roy, like Didier Gaspard, was a locksmith, though now the locksmith was the accused and not the victim. In two of the three cases discussed so far, the dire needs have been reflected in interactions between laborers and the Black colonial population.

Furthermore, throughout the notarized documents, the African woman who had possession of Chapron's stockings is referred to as "the negress wife of Le Roy."[18] *Métissage* is a word for the mixing of cultures, but in colonial French society it meant an interracial relationship. These relationships were heavily discouraged by the local church authorities.[19] In less than a year from the Le Roys being accused of theft, the new Code Noir coauthored by Bienville would make marriages between white and Black settlers (*blanche* and *noir*) illegal. Métissage represented a breakdown of traditional French values, and the royal authorities treated it as a threat. Even more so, the documents regarding the burglary possess striking clarity in stating that the couple is married. When Anne Mony is discussed later in the chapter, Madame Mony is almost always described using her own surname and not that of her husband. As soon as it was clear to the French authorities that the two had a marital relationship, those authorities were sure to account for Monsieur Le Roy's "negress wife" at every juncture.

The final disposition of the Le Roys is unknown. We can be relatively sure that the Monsieur Le Roy who appears as a local official in the 1740s is a different man from the locksmith who engaged in métissage in 1723. No records exist for Madame Le Roy, but if the coming Code Noir of 1724 were any indication, she and her husband were not likely to be let off the hook. Royal authorities had a different set of punishments they could use to control free Africans who found themselves in a vulnerable position. Theft is not a crime that a free African could be re-enslaved for according to the 1724 Code Noir. But if Monsieur Le Roy was arrested, imprisoned or indentured as punishment and Madame Le Roy was left without a means to provide for herself, she would have been in grave danger of re-enslavement. Debt was a dangerous prospect for any woman in France, let alone a lone African freewoman in the colonies. And lest we forget, what Monsieur and Madame Le Roy were accused of stealing in court, threatening to ruin their lives, were some silk stockings and a set of silverware.

The burglaries in 1723 point to the desperate conditions that the population labored under and the needs-based nature of the crimes. The cases of Marie Simon Lespronne, Didier Gaspard and Andre and Monsieur and Madame LaRoy all show that this wave of burglaries centered on procuring simple material goods that were scarce. The Didier Gaspard burglary in Gentilly, allegedly perpetrated by an enslaved African, was resolved by the alleged victim's peers well before the attorney general or his men arrived. Andre, an enslaved African, was accused of stealing sundries: linen and soap being the most notable of the items stolen. The case of Marie Lespronne, opened in the same month, involved the young woman allegedly stealing linen for her nursing stepmother from a wealthier property owner. And the Le Roys' case also involved the stealing of linen and sundries, this time allegedly done by a husband-and-wife duo. One of the main takeaways from the burglaries in 1723 is the unified nature of their participants and their goals. Relating back to our two underlying principles for understanding colonial French crime, geography and need, these crimes fall squarely inside of the methodology. In matters of geography, all three cases occurred during one of the hottest parts of the year, when temperatures average between eighty-six and ninety-two degrees Fahrenheit.[20] They also occur either within the colonial holding of New Orleans itself or in the near frontier regions like Gentilly, which was little-populated wilderness in the 1720s. Matters of need also shine through. Each case involved necessities that the climate of Louisiana demands. Nursing mothers and the enslaved alike wanted for basic hygiene products. Soap and linen are two products that the colonial regime could not produce on their own, and those supplies would have to come over by boat from France. If one person within a single year had stolen linen and soap from a property owner, it would be hard to draw conclusions from the event. But if five and more people are accused of burglary over the same items within a four-month span, it speaks to the unmet needs of colonists.

Who these alleged criminals were as a class speaks to the hierarchical, imperial methods of property distribution. Those who had, had. And those who had not, had not. All three cases involve those who fall squarely in the "had not" category and its victims are those who "had." The victims were propertied men, and the alleged perpetrators were enslaved Africans, free Africans, married couples without much property to speak of and stepdaughters. Across the three cases, all three centered on procuring different textile goods. Marie Simon was accused of stealing "linen goods" for her stepmother, while the Le Roys, were accused, in part, of stealing silk stockings. The Le Roys were also accused of stealing basic necessities like table knives. None of these accused burglars had avarice in their hearts. Each of them stole a necessity for the time and place. Marie Simon's stepmother was likely motivated by wet nursing a new child. The LeRoys sought to build a home together under extreme conditions. All of these cases, placed within their historical context, attest to the needs-based nature of crime in the early decade of colonial Louisiana.

Anne Mony and the Marine Abduction Plot

The 1723 Marine Abduction Plot casts the fraying social bonds into sharp relief. In July 1723, a young man named Marin Lafontaine confessed to knowledge of a plot to steal a large boat in the port of New Orleans. Lafontaine was born in Versailles, the seat of the French kingdom, and was little more than a young soldier stationed in the Louisiana colonies. Marin accused Anne Mony and her husband, Jean Caron, a baker in the colony of New Orleans, of leading a conspiracy of a dozen people to steal the *Ste. Elizabeth* and escape to Carolina. Lafontaine accused Anne Mony of enticing him to join the plot "five or six" days earlier.[21] And while it may seem odd for a potential rebel to go recruiting among the king's soldiers, they would have been essential for the job. The French saw it necessary to protect a mere four pirogues with twenty soldiers when going up the Mississippi. Going along the Gulf coast would have been no less dangerous.[22] From the records of the interrogation of Lafontaine, it seems that the colonial regime had reason to suspect there was a plan afoot. The investigation of the affair was an in-house operation. The initial interrogator of record is Jean-Bernard Verschars de Terrepuy, a senior aide to the colonial regime, who had been ordered by the Chevalier de Louboy to investigate the matter. Lafontaine was a soldier in the Chevalier de Louboy's company, which was stationed in the Louisiana territory at the time.

But as these stories often go, the doe-eyed soldier from Versailles named names, and the plot began to unravel. Lafontaine was the first to point the finger at Anne Mony. On August 17, a fifer in the same company named Pierre Chauvin alleged that Anne Mony had attempted to recruit him and that Jean Caron and a third man named François Millat were leading the conspiracy.[23] At this point, the investigation stalled. One way or another, the colonial authorities were able to wrangle Millat into an interrogation on September 22. He denied everything, of course.[24] But the administrative apparatus had a vested interest in crushing this threat. The next day, the counselor called all witnesses into the court, and official court proceedings began by September 24.

French colonial courts appear to have been quite different from our modern conception of courts. On the day that witnesses were called in for official review, each witness was reinterrogated individually. Jean Caron denied even thinking about desertion or disloyalty.[25] Millat and Mony both denied everything as well. After interrogations came the confrontation process. Anne Mony was escorted by armed guards into a room with her accusers. This would have already sent sparks flying as the accused and the accuser were forced to face each other in search of truth, but it seems that the pressure got to François Millat and he broke. It is impossible to know what exact event precipitated his switch, but when Attorney General Fleuriau ordered the confrontation of witnesses, Millat was among the number with Chauvin declaring that Anne Mony was behind the affair.

Anne Mony was increasingly revealed to be at the center of the plot and was quite indignant about the entire affair.[26] While her exact words are lost to history, she seems to have launched a significant defense of the accused based on ideas of legal rights that would have been novel and enlightened to the 1720s French mind.[27] Jean Caron stood by his wife the entire time, and

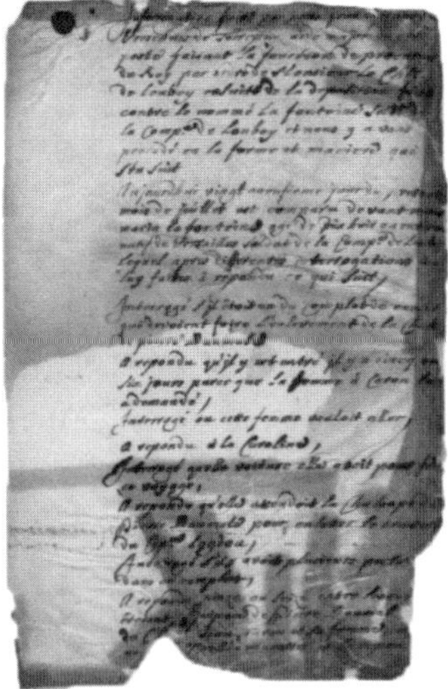

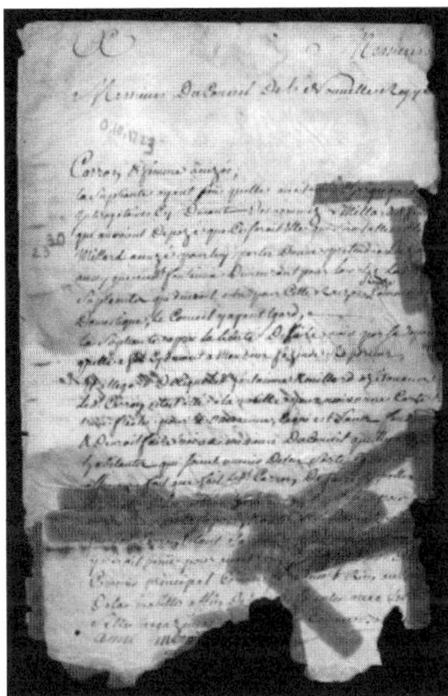

Left: The examination of Marin Lafontaine led directly to the arrest of Jean Carron, his wife, and the defeat of the Marine Abduction Plot. Here it is recorded in the notarized record. *Provided by the Louisiana Colonial Document Digitization Project # 1723-07-29-02 (13).*

Right: Jean Carron and Anne Mony pleaded that the court's procedures are unjust. Of course, of the two of them, only Anne Mony signed the notarized transcription of their protest. *Provided by the Louisiana Colonial Document Digitization Project # 1723-10-10-01 (14).*

they seem to have suffered under arrest together. But at every turn, Anne Mony is named as the recruiter and the mouthpiece for the plotters. Others were identified as potential plotters and interrogated, but the focus from that point on was on Anne Mony and her husband. It is interesting that a colonial French woman, a rarity in that time and place, could be so instrumental in organizing a large number of people on such an audacious plan and then brazenly defended the legal rights of the conspirators.

The episode exemplifies the swiftness and thoroughness with which the law could act if it needed to. A boat being stolen and escaping to an English colony would have presented a significant threat to the French legal order within Louisiana. There is no resolution to this drama within the surviving legal records. At best, Anne Mony and Jean Caron were imprisoned for a length of time and sent elsewhere within the French empire. At worst, they were executed. But it is easy to see how the desperate conditions that de Charlevoix noted in his journal could have spawned a dire plot to escape to the English colonies, where the land was drier, the seasons more temperate and the markets freer and supplies far more abundant than French Louisiana.

The Bad Bread Mutiny of 1745

Anne Mony was not the only person causing the most severe forms of trouble for the French colonial authorities. The same kinds of unfulfilled needs that drove Marie Lespronne to burgle her fellow settlers persisted for decades through the Basse-Louisiane region. Twenty-two years after Anne Mony's marine abduction plot was foiled by a greenhorn cadet from Versailles, the French continued to experience unrest from within the colony. The re-creation of European society, with its loyal soldiers, ample supplies and landed nobility, continued to flounder into the latter half of the eighteenth century. These failures by the government resulted in a culture of disorder that penetrated deep into the ranks of the colonial military. These failures and this culture of disorder were made manifest in the Bad Bread Mutiny of 1745.

The relatively small number of garrison soldiers stationed throughout the Basse-Louisiane, small compared to the regiments in Europe at the time, found themselves subjected to the same deplorable conditions as the poorer members of Louisiana society. The soldiers existed to provide security for the colony's productive materials, the plantations, ports, ships and raw goods. Occasionally, these soldiers were deployed to deal with civilian matters, to arrest and escort prisoners primarily. But their primary goal was to serve as protectors of the colony's marketable assets. As such, the soldiers also served as slave catchers for the colony and early keepers of the social order, itself built entirely around the colony's productive capabilities. And when these soldiers stepped out of line, the French officers over them employed cruel punishments in order to control those stationed in the Louisiana colony.

The French colonial soldiers did not have access to the same supply of foods that European-based soldiers ate. In general, the French colonial soldiers partook primarily in a bread known as *le pain de munitions*, or the "munition bread." The French made munition bread out of a combination of rye and other flours. The process produced a hard, mostly nonperishable, black bread that could be served to soldiers and reliably fill their bellies. Munition bread was an unwelcome, unpleasant and dry meal. Within the Louisiana colony, it was also the only thing soldiers could depend on having served to them every day. In an environment where butter was a luxury, munition bread served as the bread *and* butter of the French regimental diet. In a way, munition bread was the order of French regimental life made manifest.

This is the official recording of the interrogation of Dominique. Ultimately, he would be the only man executed for refusing to eat the spoiled bread. *Provided by the Louisiana Colonial Document Digitization Project. # 1745-07-13-06.png (03).*

And if munition bread represented regimental life, on July 11, 1745, a soldier named Braude, who went by Dominique among his comrades, rejected that life. When Braude received his dinner allotment of blackened rye, he pulled out his knife in front of his officer, cut the bread open and then refused to eat the bread. The implication was that the bread was inedible, and Braude made that fact known to the officer over him. For Braude's refusal to eat the bread, the commanding officers had him arrested and thrown into jail. The mutiny over the quality of the bread certainly included more soldiers and even more companies of soldiers than just Braude. At least one other soldier, a man named Jean Frederic, testified to the court that he also refused to eat the bread. And another witness to the incident, Jean Biat "Lauvergne," testified to the judicial council that multiple regiments refused the bread but the trouble started with Braude in Gauvrit's company. Braude claimed that two others advised him to refuse the bread, though the judicial council confronted only one man, Julian Bidaux, on the count of advising Braude. Monsieur Bidaux widely denied those charges, and Braude remained the only man arrested for the mutinous meal.

The mutiny represented a perfect challenge to the colonial order. Colonial leaders decided that deviant behavior as petty as demanding better bread represented a dire threat to their way of life. Braude's commanding officer marched him to jail on July 11. On July 12, Mayor de Benac, the mayor of New Orleans at the time, sent a petition to the judicial council to open prosecution against Braude immediately and requested that the man be tried with "prejudice." The judicial council agreed, appointed Mayor de Benac as the prosecutor for the case and made haste with the trial. On July 13, a parade of soldiers from Braude's company confronted him with their testimony in front of a panel composed of colonial officials. Ultimately, Braude provided the most damning evidence himself. A few days earlier, on noticing that the munition bread was inedible, Braude himself said, "What—no bread? We must then make war." His own words sealed his fate.

The judicial council held the weight of a man's life in their hands, so they concluded the interrogations to ponder the evidence and return the next day to deliver the sentence. On July 14, three days after Braude refused to eat the munition bread, thereby demanding better conditions for soldiers in the colony, the soldier was condemned to be shot in the town square until dead. The judicial council made note that Braude's comrades in arms, who were his fellow mutineers and the ones who put him up to the task of refusing the bread, should watch him be shot in the town square. On that same day, the judicial council made another ruling, which stood in direct contrast to the previous sentencing: Braude should be hanged in the public square. The contradiction at the end of the record is puzzling, and the French judicial council felt no further need to explain themselves. They did not notarize a record of Braude's death, only his two execution orders. There is no record about whether the confusion about his execution comes from the trial haste or the consternation of his fellow soldiers in being forced to watch their comrade brutally shot to death for refusing dinner. It could be either or some third thing—perhaps bullets were in low supply that day and thus Braude had to die by the rope and not the gun.

Laborde, Pontuel and a Fistful of Livres

Though murders on the frontier have a personal nature, always with gigantic colonial personalities screaming through the dull tones of centuries-old notarized letters, they also revolve around the same needs that drive all colonial life. Cash, royal banknotes called *livres* and other forms of paper money that floated around the colonies, was an important resource. Paper money represented an escape from the barter economy and fixed forms of wealth that dominated, and subjugated, much of the colony's population. Land, cash crops and investment wealth represented only one's business investments in the colonies. And despite a few landed white Creoles who sought to put down roots, the point of investing in the colony was to make enough capital to leave the colony and retire in the metropole's more temperate climate. Even the Sieur de Bienville, the colony's father if there ever was one, spent his twenty-four-year retirement in Paris, advocating for the colony from a great distance and more comfortable environs.

Back then, as now, men were willing to die over a handful of paper bank notes. On November 17, 1722, an inspector for the French colonial authorities named Guilhet interrogated a French fisherman named Charles Desmercier Ecuyer Laborde, or Laborde for short. The interrogation was over the death of another fisherman named Pontuel. Laborde reported that

The Louisiana Historical Society's work in the early twentieth century stands as a colossus in colonial document preservation. Without their hard work, many of these documents would be unusable today. *Provided by the Louisiana Colonial Document Digitization Project # 1722-11-17-01.French.png(05).*

he owed Pontuel forty livres, a sum of money that would have likely fed either of the men for a year,[28] and Pontuel threatened Laborde to either pay him the money or quit the colony. At a later interrogation on December 23 of the same year, Laborde offered more details. This time, Laborde faced a new inspector, a man named Arnaud Bonnaud, since Inspector Guilhet had died in the meantime. Laborde explained that Pontuel had hounded him to leave the colony via Lake Pontchartrain and then beat him with an oar in the stomach, left to fish and returned to find Laborde still in New Orleans. At this point, Pontuel pulled a gun on Laborde, certainly a powder-style flintlock, and said, "You will be my tenth," before attempting to fire the gun at Laborde. When the gun did not go off, Laborde wrestled it from Pontuel and shot the man.[29]

The story of Laborde and the murder of Pontuel shows how individual relations between subjects of the Crown were strained under scarce resources, hard work and the lack of government presence. Laborde was charged with killing Pontuel after admitting to the deed on November 17, 1722. In this case, two fishermen on the frontier come to a violent disagreement over the sum of forty livres (enough to nearly feed a man for a year). The resolutions offered by Pontuel, the aggressor, were for Laborde to pay him the sum or flee the colony. Laborde was not intimidated, and the two wrestled until Pontuel was shot and killed. The sort of negotiations we see in the Louisiana frontier were short, violent and quick. While nothing is known of Laborde's prior associations, Pontuel's demands boil down to the simplest expressions of resolution: either give me what I am owed or get away. Violence seems to be a normal tool in these cases. Pontuel claimed to have killed nine others when he threatened Laborde, and Laborde seemed entirely unwilling to change his actions until Pontuel threatened murder. Laborde's matter appears to have been the least interesting case the Superior Council had in front of them at the time. The case went cold for months in the middle, and at the end, Laborde was neither convicted nor punished for killing Pontuel in self-defense. It could be that the Superior Council did

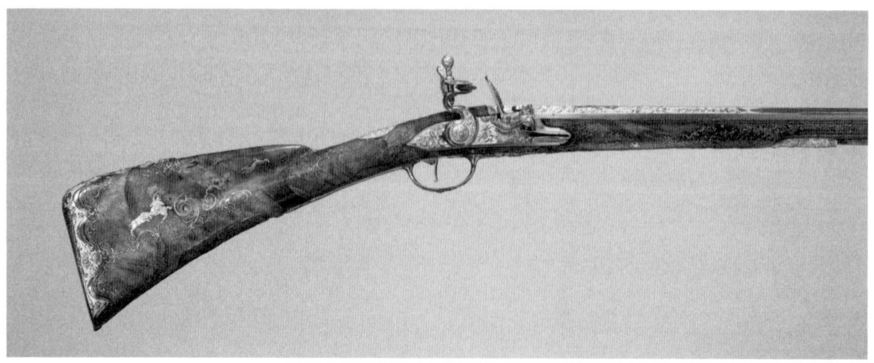

Eighteenth-century guns were constructed of hardwood and iron. When the powder became wet, or the gun was too cumbersome to reload, the heft of the guns made them suitable bludgeons. In the story of Pontuel and Laborde, a hardwood and iron gun similar to the far more pristine rifle above would have delivered the fatal blow. *Image provided by the Metropolitan Museum and the Harris Brisbane Dick and Rogers Funds, 1987.*

not concern itself with the murder of murderers. It could also be that what happened out in the marshes stayed there. Certainly, the Superior Council did not see any profit in pursuing the truth of the matter to its end.

We can see various instances of the legal system breaking down in this case. Pontuel and Laborde were far away from New Orleans for the fatal altercation, so Laborde left Pontuel's body at Ville aux Chats. The investigation took months to make very little progress, as the only follow-up was in December of the same year. And between the first and second interrogations, the investigator assigned to the matter died due to unrelated circumstances, likely the effects of the Louisiana climate, medical problems arising from colonization or old age.

Conclusions

The notarial records present a somewhat bleak picture of New Orleans, especially at the dawn of the French colonial era. However, as people who undertook an incredibly daunting task or had that task forced on them by the courts and slavers, the settlers and the enslaved who carved a city out of the subtropical mire deserve their accolades. Plantation slaves, convicts sent across the ocean, locksmiths, sailors, soldiers, the Natives who cooperated with them and the wives who managed their affairs all struggled to build a society that would sit atop the mud. To offer a different perspective on the time and place, for the few thousand at most residents of the Louisiana territory, it could very well be that the crime rate was remarkably low for the circumstances. And this possibility paints a sunnier picture—that among the many unwanted Frenchmen and women cast upon the Gulf Shore, the vast majority of them learned to live with one another, trade and learn, tolerate and then intermarry and eventually become one people. Given the census numbers of the era, either many crimes and disagreements did not make it to the Superior Council, the records did not survive, or only the lower-class and enslaved colonists experienced enough hardship to be pushed toward "petty" crime. If that is the case, then the Superior Council got involved only, and thus recorded those crimes, when those petty crimes threatened the status of the wealthier, powerful elite. It is possible there was something of a mix—that fellow got along with their fellow and most disagreements were handled far away from soldiers and magistrates. Those stories are lost to the mud.

Crime might have happened to the plantation-owning upper crust of the Louisiana colony, but the consequences for crimes went almost entirely to the townspeople of New Orleans and the outlying regions. The lower classes, especially the landless whites who practiced a trade, bore the majority of the punishment for any given crime. We cannot say that the courts in New France operated entirely on the basis of wealth and class. The Superior Council cared about transplanting useful precedents from the Old World and crafting new precedents to suit the New World. Good order also had to be maintained, and that meant a government that conformed to the minimal requirements of that age. The king's presence needed to be felt, especially among the upper crust of society. Men like Fleuriau, Vaudreuil and Bienville wanted to feel safe in the colony. They wanted profit and glory. The kingdom of France served as their vessel to extract wealth, profit, glory and even security from the New World. For the landless whites, the government needed them only to deal in the king's money and pay the king's taxes. As long as they played their small part in the grand design of New France, the middling people of New France could muddle along unhindered and resolve disagreements on their own. But when the upper crust needed to feel safe and insulated from the artisans and farmers and sailors, the Superior Council served to hand down control and punishment on behalf of the French empire.

Without laying too much blame at the feet of the few Frenchmen who schemed New France and its colonies into being, a few fundamental features of New France meant that crime would be ever present and basically unsolvable: the expanse of territory, the climate and environment and the way the colony was run. The vast expanse of the territory meant that no single administrator could ever hope to spread the king's law equally and effectively. In time, royal governors like Vaudreuil began to argue with one another over whether Canada or Orleans would exploit the vast Mississippian interior. Most of the French settlers deep in the interior lived as far away from New Orleans and Versailles as physically possible. For the *petit blancs*, "small whites," in the interior of New France, the Superior Council, the royal governor, even the king of France meant little to their day-to-day lives. In colonial Haiti, petit blancs were those white colonists who either did not have any land or property or had comparatively little compared to the big whites. For the small hold settlers, the local contract-holder for exploiting the land, usually granted by royal governors to profit-seeking entrepreneurs, meant far more than a distant governor of noble descent. The vast expanse of New France meant that the contract holders representing the government in an area could go largely unchecked in their power.

The environment itself likely pushed many of the colonists into a point of desperation. The heat and the humidity contributed to many of the crimes that occurred in colonial Louisiana. The subtropical heat and swampy climate meant that many of the crops Europeans relied on simply did not grow well along the Gulf Coast. The French were so set on finding precious metals to exploit in the interior of the continent, they never realized the wealth of soil they had captured. No matter where you found yourself in New France, food was either scarce, hard-won or expensive. The heat and humidity differed from chilly, windy Brittany and sunny, placid Bordeaux. Hurricanes ravaged the Gulf South and contributed to the unreliable shipments of goods from the Caribbean colonies. Bienville practically had to beg before he could import the first slaves into the colony. The settlers desperately wanted to offload the impossible task of settlement onto cheap, replaceable souls. The hard work of settlement, of building and mining, dredging and farming, fell to enslaved Native Americans and enslaved Africans. For the enslaved, New France consisted of unforgivable tyranny. But any crime that the enslaved committed was immediately a high crime of its own class because it threatened the essential structure of the colony—the slave must labor without question. The next chapter deals with the crimes of and against the enslaved.

Finally, the way the French ran Louisiana contributed immensely to their own problems controlling the colony. The so-called mutiny over bad bread and Anne Mony's plot to steal a boat and escape New France could have been avoided by the French kingdom, the royal governor, the

Superior Council or any other official with the power to make the lives of the soldiers better. Instead, the soldiers were given *pain d'ammunition*, which would be literally translated as "gun bread" and could not have tasted much better than what the name implies. The soldiers were used as slave catchers, guards and the first line of defense against any Native American raids. When the soldiers did step toward freedom, the Superior Council swiftly arrested conspirators. Any soldier, sailor or merchant who rebelled against the empire could have been executed. The third chapter of the book explores the money crises that plagued New France, which could be linked to the resource scarcity and desperation behind crimes like the murder of Pontuel, the 1723 burglaries and the Marie Lespronne case.

If there are any lessons for the contemporary reader in these stories, they lie in the underlying causes. Perhaps these causes have not been addressed. After reading these stories, I hope the reader feels a pull to make common cause with others in looking around at their own environment, the laws governing their lives and the accessibility of their surroundings. The history of these valiant, defiant people should light a spark within the reader. Otherwise, the writer has told their stories in vain.

2

THE CODE NOIR

During the latter part of the eighteenth century, the entire kingdom of France devolved into bloody revolution over many of the issues that colonists had been feeling for a century before the people of the kingdom revolted. We can sense something of Anne Mony in the impulses that led to the French Revolution. The people of France were well and truly done with this government that seemed to care only for the pockets of the king and not the health of the kingdom or its people. From that revolution would spawn important documents in the history of liberal governance like the Declaration of the Rights of Man. In the inferno of the dying ancien régime and the height of the Reign of Terror, Maximilien Robespierre abolished slavery across all France, including the colonies and the territories. The French government's abolishment of slavery in 1794 occurred seventy years after the Crown instituted the Louisiana Code Noir in 1724. Along with the Declaration of the Rights of Man and the Citizen, the Louisiana Code Noir is one of the most infamous documents produced by eighteenth-century France and perhaps one of the most infamous legal codes of all time.

There is no way we can address the topic of crime in colonial Louisiana without addressing the crime of human slavery. Though slavery was not a crime in early eighteenth-century France, today slavery is recognized as a crime against humanity that cannot be countenanced on any terms. A survey of crime in New France would not be complete without understanding the institution of slavery. And even further, within New France the institution of slavery was by far the most influential colonial social, political and economic institution. The era of French dominion over Louisiana was never known for its strong, steadfast government or tight military control. But the chattel slavery perpetrated against Africans in the eighteenth century touched on the foundations of every other institution in colonial life. From the homestead to the plantation and even to the church, all reckoned with slavery. Most would seek to profit off the institution. And voices of dissent were few and far between.

Then, if we are dealing with the paradox of a "legal crime" in the context of slavery within French Louisiana, we must seek to understand how this influential institution was regulated and how those regulations played out within the colonies. This area of research is known as state crime, and it provides a way for us to read through the history of the Code Noir and produce a structured understanding. In this sense, the story of the Code Noir is the story of the subjugation of entire peoples for the profit of colonial landlords. But the point of the research into the Code Noir is to better understand the ways in which the French regime was trying to regulate an important institution and the ways in which the French regime was trying to solidify social institutions that already existed before 1724. In understanding the history, we can understand that the Code Noir is a founding document of American racism. The Code Noir became the basis for many of the racist institutions that plagued the American South at least until the Civil War. The ways in which French masters coerced slaves into toiling across the Gulf South grew into the institutions that were used to terrorize African American populations during the period of U.S. slavery in Louisiana and beyond.

The Introduction of Slavery to the Gulf South

From the beginning, neglect in search of profit served as the central moral axis for the French slaveholder. The French colonial administration and the slave traders dealing in human cargo gravely mismanaged the importation of European slavery to French Louisiana to disastrous effect. The colonists were desperate for slaves to do necessary work for little to no cost and certainly without the cost of a wage. Bienville himself took charge in ensuring that African slaves were imported into the colony as soon as possible. Some early enslaved Africans no doubt dotted the landscape of the Gulf South before that point. But when Bienville began pushing for the importation of slaves, the slave trade's full force of impact came to the Gulf South. The first mass shipments of enslaved Africans began arriving in 1719. Colonists sent their agents into the slave-laden Caribbean with instructions to buy enslaved Africans with specific trade knowledge, the knowledge of growing rice, and meeting certain physical standards. Bienville and the landlords had no illusions about the benefits of enslaved labor. Enslaved labor would bring cheap, necessary skills and labor into the economy, and if the swamp, heat or disease took them, more could be bought.

And the lack of enslaved labor for the colonies in the early and middle seventeenth century was not for want of trying. The early years of French Canada developed métissage, a form of sex slavery whereby Native women served as concubines and commodities for fur traders and settlers. When the colonial administrators opened French Louisiana to settlement, and even earlier when the Acadians immigrated into the middle-south of Louisiana, Canadian immigrants brought the practice of métissage with them. Some of the tribes were willing to engage in the slave trade with the Europeans. But the French plantation owners found enslaved Native Americans to be unwieldy. The enslaved Natives knew the land, had those of shared culture nearby and often escaped. Because of this, the French plantation owners who wished to emulate the great plantations of the Caribbean quickly began to desire enslaved Africans. As enslaved Africans arrived weak from travel and lost in a new land, plantation owners, merchants and people of all social levels found them to be far easier to exploit.

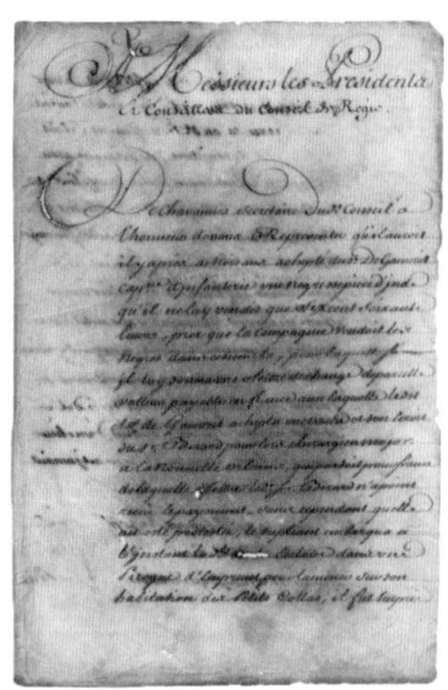

A record of a dispute between colonists over the price and sale of an African slave. When the slave ran away, the purchaser sued the seller. The French system of slavery robbed Africans of their humanity and replaced it with commodity value. *Provided by the Louisiana Colonial Document Digitization Project # 1725-04-10-04 (15).*

The settlers in colonial Louisiana desired slaves for their capacity to perform hard labor without the need to supply them with excess food, supplies and wealth. The development of slavery was intertwined with the environment of French Louisiana. French settlers wanted to displace the excess stress of the harsh, swampy terrain and oppressive climate onto other people. In Europe, this labor would have been offloaded from landlords onto peasants and serfs. But the New World analogue of the peasant servant, the indentured servant, turned out to be an ill-suited tool for the hard labor of taming the Caribbean and the Gulf Coast.

White indentured servants had rights and were protected under French laws. They could not be made to work until exhaustion for little good. They could not be deprived of necessities for profit. Some could, and even did, sue other members of French society for mistreatment. And if these indentured servants or their children managed to buy land and begin cultivating it, they could command their own wealth. The victims of colonial chattel slavery, on the other hand, were disposable. French law mostly neglected to protect slaves. Enslaved people could not own wealth. They could not buy their own land or earn independence through learning a trade. The landlords of the French New World victimized the untold masses of enslaved Native Americans and Africans, in part, simply because there was a need and they were allowed to do so.

Justifying Slavery in "Free" France

Modern students of history can tend toward excusing slavers on the grounds that they did not know better. This line of reasoning falls into the trap of viewing slavery as something retroactively criminal and unethical. In reality, French society had a long and deep understanding of slavery as a moral ill. And more to the point, the absolute devastation that enslaved populations experienced in New France would have been an unmissable phenomenon. During the eighteenth century, the French identified their national character with the ideas of liberty, rights and privileges, or at the least the tension between those things and an overbearing dynasty. In practice, it seems at first glance that the French did not keep many enslaved peoples in their motherland. It is likely that French slaves and free Africans combined to form around .025 percent of the French population during the era. But however close the French psyche might have clung to the idea of there being no enslaved peoples in France, this did not dissuade French settlers and French slavers from buying and trading in human captives. Something about the journey across the Atlantic Ocean washed away the inherent sins of slavery. Some essential characteristic of the colonies let the settlers rationalize chattel ownership of people.

The trouble began with the fact that the realities of the New World and the realities of France did not line up. This divide was meaningful and profound. Within France, the folk understanding of slavery held plainly that there was no slavery in France. For many Frenchmen, their understanding was that in 1315, King Louis X had outlawed slavery by royal decree, rendering all further details on the ownership of people moot. However, as the middle ages turned into the modern age and the pious monarchs of the medieval period turned into the new monarchs and absolutists of the eighteenth centuries, slavery became an increasing necessity in the competition between colonia empires for economic and military power. But even during this period, the sense of France's freedom was so thorough that in 1571 and 1691, two separate incidents occurred in which the governments of France freed enslaved Africans that had been brought into the kingdom to be bought and sold.[30]

This is a momentous departure from the common narrative that Europeans of previous centuries held slavery to a different moral standard than we do today. In 1571, the people of Bordeaux prevented the sale of recently imported slaves, and the parliament local to the area freed the slaves outright. And then later, and far closer to our narrative, the minister of the marine, a supervisor of colonial enterprises for the king, declared that all slaves that made their way to France would be freed. That the minister of the marine, the primary agent of managing the colonial economies that relied so thoroughly on enslaved labor, would issue a proclamation declaring for the emancipation of enslaved Africans in France is stunning. It shows how complex the relationship between the French and slavery had become by 1691. It is without question that the French government endorsed a brutal form of chattel slavery in New France. But one gets the sense that the French were aware they were playing with fire, and stripping a man of his rights only paves the path for yours to be stripped away.

Thus, slavery within the French world created a legal, philosophical and generational divide that defined a generation of colonial legal scholars and colonial policy. Throughout the eighteenth century, French high society was defined by the attention it paid to the arts, secular philosophy, reading and early naturalism. To be a legal scholar was to be well read in the Enlightened philosophy of the time. The French colonial elite identified most with Montesquieu, and the reason why is quite clear. Montesquieu provided the most significant loophole for the French colonists to justify slavery within the French traditions of freedom and Enlightenment. This justification was called the *moeur*, and it can be translated roughly as referring to the traditions of a place, culture or geographic area. Through the construct of the moeur, colonists would find the way to justify their possession of enslaved people of Enlightened, fashionable, legal grounds.

Montesquieu could not square the circle of the "no slaves in France" mindset with the reality of chattel slavery, but he did offer a form of deference to the colonial regimes whose effects would be wide ranging and devastating. For in defending colonial France's system of slavery, Montesquieu argued, and soon after the colonial elites all the more vehemently, that the customs (moeurs) of the colonial holdings overwrote the need to enforce French social distinctions that could not function because of the climate of the region.[31] The moeur provided an excuse for colonial plantation owners to justify their embrace of slavery within French society, and it allowed the French intellectual class that resided within continental Europe to wash their hands of the matter entirely.

Introducing the Code Noir

All that was left for the government agents, stockholders and colonial landowners was to find a way to regulate slavery so that it might be sustainable and turn a profit for the landowners and the king. The first attempt at Versailles to regulate slavery, the colonies and international trade came in the 1680s. The kingdom felt that local French administrators were not enforcing the laws of the kingdom well enough, and the Code Noir of 1685 was an attempt to create a legal system that was suitable for sustaining an empire that needed slavery to function. The Code Noir of 1685 was the first attempt by the court of King Louis XIV, sometimes known to history as the Sun King, to regulate slavery. He built the same palace of Versailles that his successor, Louis XV, would issue his edict on notarized colonial documents from. Indeed, the whole period of French history defined by noblemen ruling from sunny, temperate, pleasant, forested Versailles begins with King Louis XIV. In 1685, as the French Crown began to reckon with the debt caused by Louis XIV's *mageste* and warmongering, the court issued the Code Noir as a way to codify French colonial slave society. The aim was sustainability. The French Caribbean was especially profitable for the kingdom. Slavery was recognized as a necessity to make the sugar industry function, and thus it needed to be controlled so that enough enslaved Africans in good enough condition to labor would flow into the colonies. All for the production of sugar.

The authors of the Code Noir decided that the best way to control slaves was to control the actions of people within the colonies. This was done for two main reasons, both of which are readily apparent in the text of the code. The first was to ensure that the colonial projects retained a Catholic and French nature. So long as the colonies remained Catholic in religion and

French in culture, the courtiers at Versailles hoped the colonists would remain loyal to Paris. The second reason the authors of the Code Noir wanted to control the actions of the colonists was to create a defined hierarchy that would permanently separate the interests of slaveholders from that of the slaves. So long as slaves and enslavers were divided and free Frenchman divided from enslaved Africans, the threat of a general colonial uprising was suppressed. The edicts in the 1684 Code Noir break down into these two broad categories: edicts meant to ensure that the slave-based colonies remained Catholic and French and edicts meant to ensure that slavery's brutal code remained in force.

The 1685 Code Noir is a relic of early French colonization and a puzzling document that is, at times, as confusing as it is cruel. It is the unrefined seed that would blossom into the infamous Code Noir of 1724. Compared to the 1724 version, the Code Noir of 1685 is confused and disorganized. It reads like an ad hoc list of penalties addressing paranoias specific to the royal court, colonial officials and plantation owners. The 1685 Code contains fifty-nine provisions covering everything from the penalty on masters for having extramarital relations with a slave that results in children to the minimum nourishment requirements for slaves due from their masters. There is no real sense of organization to the document, a trait that it shares with the Code of 1724. It meanders from one topic to the next, doing its best to group them based on the actions the Code sought to formalize or prohibit. And in a strange twist, the 1724 and the 1685 versions share the same opening article: that the colonies would be French and Catholic and that Jews were banned from immigrating to the colonies.

The 1724 update to the Code rationalized the code so that it was easier to enforce. However, between the two documents, the central logic remains unchanged. Across all of the provisions in the 1685 edicts, the only way to forge legal bonds between enslaver and enslaved person was through marriage in the Catholic Church. Congregations of enslaved peoples under any circumstances were to be forbidden and punished. There was to be no concubinage, no métissage, no familial connections between enslaver and enslaved person outside of the French and Catholic way. And even then, it would be between master and freed slave, raising free children. Never would a free Frenchman, Creole or otherwise, be allowed to live in marriage with an enslaved person. The Crown sought to separate white, French and free from African, Native and enslaved, except outside of the strictest of social institutions like the Catholic Church. For all of these reasons, the Code Noir stands as a founding document of American racism. From segregation to the separation of the justice system to vigilante crime against African Americans, the patterns set into place by the Code Noir continue to persist in American culture.

In tracing this history, the one provision that stands out as a poignant example of the perniciousness of the Code Noir of 1685 is Article 1, section 16. This part of the 1685 Code sought to lay out that slaves from different masters holding any sort of meeting, congregation or grouping, including marriages, was strictly forbidden. Within this provision, it lays out the punishments for these sorts of congregations. For participating in an unsanctioned meeting, the French authorities would punish the slaves with beatings, branding with the fleur-de-lis on the face and execution. For the slaveholders of New France, much like slaveholders in any time and place, enslaved people congregating and speaking to one another on their own terms was a paramount risk. Those meetings inevitably led to slave revolt.

In the face of the existential threat of the slave revolt, the writers of the Code Noir took an extraordinary step. The provision against slave congregations goes on to deputize "subjects" to "approach the offenders, to arrest them and take them to prison, even if they are not officers and there is not yet any decree against them."[32] By order of Versailles and carried out through the governing council of the colonies, subjects of the Crown, being taxpayers of all kinds, propertied or unpropertied, were each and every one to be watchers of the enslaved population. Here, we see an admission that the state was inadequate to fully uphold slavery. In order for such an intense system of racial segregation and suppression to take hold, it would take police actions and violence from a broad swath of the population. That same population of subjects who were not to marry slaves, not to do business with them outside of a master's permission, were now tasked with the violent, extrajudicial repression of the enslaved meetings. By 1724, the system of vigilante action by non-deputized subjects of the Crown was well entrenched and likely spread to enforcement beyond slave gatherings. The hierarchy set to paper in 1685 firmly established the power of the slaveholding society over that of the slave, in conjunction with the Church, and set no rules on how to resolve the so-called crimes of enslaved people besides setting clear maximum punishments: flogging, dismemberment, branding with the fleur-de-lis and summary execution. Vigilantism against African Americans in the American South morphed into the notorious lynch mobs that terrorized African Americans for hundreds of years. Of course, these lynchings would often be dismissed as local to the South, a result of their culture, essentially a moeur in all but name, and thus excused. In 1685, we can see one of the deepest roots of the hanging tree burrow into the land.

With an understanding that mob justice was sanctioned to quell slave gatherings, and an implicit admission that subjects of the Crown would be necessary as actors in the enforcement of slavery, the behaviors of white, propertied subjects in the cases of Didier Gaspard's burglary and the Le Roys come into sharper focus. In the case of the burglary, the boat captain François Rilieux took it upon himself to detain Andre, an enslaved man, the moment Andre was caught with goods that he should not possess. He then brought Andre to a nearby landowner so that they could discover the root of the alleged crime and act as arbiters of the king's law. The arrival of a royal official essentially meant that the story of the propertied men became the story with an official, notarized signature. And the frustrating lack of evidence as to how slaves were punished begins to act more like the unifying aspect of each case. The Code Noir made the punishment of slaves routine and delegated to the master of the slave. So long as a slave was whipped, branded, mutilated or executed within legal limits, and nobody registered a complaint over maltreatment, then it hardly bore writing down.

What follows is a collection of stories from colonial Louisiana that appear in the notarized colonial records. All of these stories are connected in a significant way to the various articles of the Code Noir of 1724. The stories of Andre and Chapron have been touched on in the earlier chapter, but they are worth looking at again under the light of the Code Noir. Some of the records that appear before 1724, and thus before the implementation of the infamous 1724 code, are still worthy of revisiting and considering how life might be calcified or changed drastically when the 1724 Code was implemented. But regardless, the intent is for the reader to see how the Code Noir practically affected the lives of those subjected to its maltreatment and draw parallels to the maltreatment of various people throughout North American history.

Article VI: Marriage Under the Code Noir

We forbid our white subjects of either sex to contract marriage with the Blacks, under penalty of punishment and an arbitrary fine; we forbid all Curates, Priests and Missionaries, secular or regular, and even Ship Chaplins, to marry them. We also forbid our white subjects, even manumitted Blacks or those born free, to live in concubinage with the slaves.

—*Article VI, Code Noir 1724*[33]

The 1685 version of the Code Noir had little to say about marriage beyond that both participants must either be married or free, and that they must be married in the Catholic way by a member of the Catholic faith.[34] However, in the 1724 Code Noir, the Parisian court and their colonial advisors, men like Bienville, inserted provisions banning the marriage of African and European people, regardless of their status as free or enslaved. The roots of this push likely had a twofold origin. First was the endless war that the Church and social conservatives waged against métissage and all other forms of miscegenation. Second, and more importantly, the French colonists wanted to institute a racial hierarchy that would preserve slavery indefinitely. In order for this to be the case, European and African stock had to be kept separate as much as possible, and no free man of any race could be allowed to enter into familial relations with an enslaved person. Slaves could not be allowed to give birth to free men, and free men could not be allowed to father slaves.

In the case of Joseph Chapron's missing silk stockings, the way court officials recorded the case displays how the 1724 Code was designed to reflect a growing cultural reality and the racial hierarchy in the colonies. The Le Roys were an interracial couple. There is no information in the documents about how the Le Roys were married and whether or how either of them had been manumitted. But because they existed on the frontier of legal acceptability, Joseph Chapron was able to act against the interracial LaRoy family with impunity to build his case. When Chapron's associate directed Chapron toward an enslaved woman, he interrogated the woman himself. Her testimony under this pressure was a deciding factor in the case. Chapron had property and social standing, and the Le Roys were working people. Chapron was a Frenchman, and the Le Roys were an interracial couple. By the order of the times, a severe power imbalance existed between the two.

Once Chapron felt confident enough to accuse the Le Roys in court, the court officials took pains to note that the Le Roys were free and married. The case occurred in 1723. But within the context of the Code Noir, especially the coming 1724 Code, recording their marriage within legal documents makes a great deal of sense. That the interracial couple were both legally free, Catholic and married was a matter of state interest. Failure to meet those qualifications would have made both of the Le Roys criminals by default. But in the climate of the mid-1720s, meeting those requirements did not offer much help. After Chapron's associate gave his deposition and Madame Le Roy returned a stocking to Chapron, the couple was arrested for interrogation and the records of the case against them go cold.

The Le Roy couple must have been living on the edge of French colonial society. We do not know if Bienville, another colonial official, a Versailles courtier, the king himself or all of them conspired to outlaw interracial marriages in the colonies. What we do know is that Joseph Chapron and the criminal courts treated the Le Roys differently than those who were not challenging the French conceptions of marriage. Their marriage could only have made the situation more difficult. Indeed, while Anne Mony's name is recorded again and again in the notarized records, the name of Monsieur Le Roy's wife is lost to time. To the French courts, she was only "the negress wife." The label is repeated again and again throughout the court proceedings, at once labeling the relationship as a *legal* concubinage while ensuring that it is recorded *differently* than any other marriage in the records.

Come the 1724 Code, it is impossible to say whether or not the Le Roy marriage would have been invalidated under the new code. In theory, divorce and annulment were impossibilities outside of specific circumstances. If the wife of Monsieur Le Roy was free and he was free and they were both Catholic and married in the Catholic Church before the promulgation of the 1724 Code, then their marriage would be secure. No record of an annulment or a divorce exists. However, after 1724, their marriage would have become an oddity and potentially a criminal liability. And as discussed before, if either Le Roy carried a criminal record, especially a branding mark as a result of a previous crime, their punishment would have been swift and severe. Madame Le Roy, in particular, would have been left especially vulnerable in the wake of a prosecution of her husband.

Free and enslaved Africans of all kinds existed under a different set of legal norms than the rest of French society. The Code Noir provided the absolute guidelines for dealing with slaves, Africans and Jews—essentially, those the French saw as the true outsiders. Meanwhile, this was not the case for the rest of colonial society. Even free Native tribes enjoyed fairer treatment by the French than those subjected to the Code Noir. White men and women, foreigners, petty and perilous criminals alike did not suffer the mouers of the Code Noir. Marie Lespronne, the girl who stole linens, was not subjected to a vigilante mob. Anne Mony, despite the severity of her crimes, was never assumed guilty because of the first testimony of the first men the investigator spoke with. A man like the settler Rivard du Vigne could block key access points through the territory, cause endless consternation and never face the prison barracks. Poor or propertied, French settlers like Rivard, Anne and Marie had some rights under the archaic French laws. Enslaved people and anyone governed by the Code Noir did not have even the presumption of rights.

Article XXXVIII: Reprimands Against Masters

> *Article XXXVIII. We also forbid our subjects in the said country, of whatever quality and condition they may be, to torture their slaves or have them tortured, under whatever pretext there may be, nor to mutilate or have mutilated any member of the body, under penalty of confiscation of the slaves, and extraordinary criminal proceedings: we permit them solely, when they believe their slaves merit it, to have them chained and flogged.*[35]

In late July 1727, an enslaved African named Choucoura was remanded by Pierre Gaulaz after having run away from his master's plantation. According to the Code Noir of 1724, the punishments recommended to Choucoura's master were flogging or branding or, if a repeated offense, a long-term flight or part of a congregation of slaves, potentially death. Choucoura belonged to the Natchez plantation, at that point owned by Sieur de Merveilleux, but command of slaves had been given to Pierre Gaulaz as part of his employment contract. Gaulaz was an overseer, a whip master whose job was to organize and control the enslaved Africans on the plantation. When an enslaved person escaped, as Choucoura did in early July of that year, it was Gaulaz's job to return the slave to the plantation. And because the French were paranoid about the danger of runaway societies in frontier territory, known as maroons, soldiers were sent to help Gaulaz return the slave to the Natchez plantation.

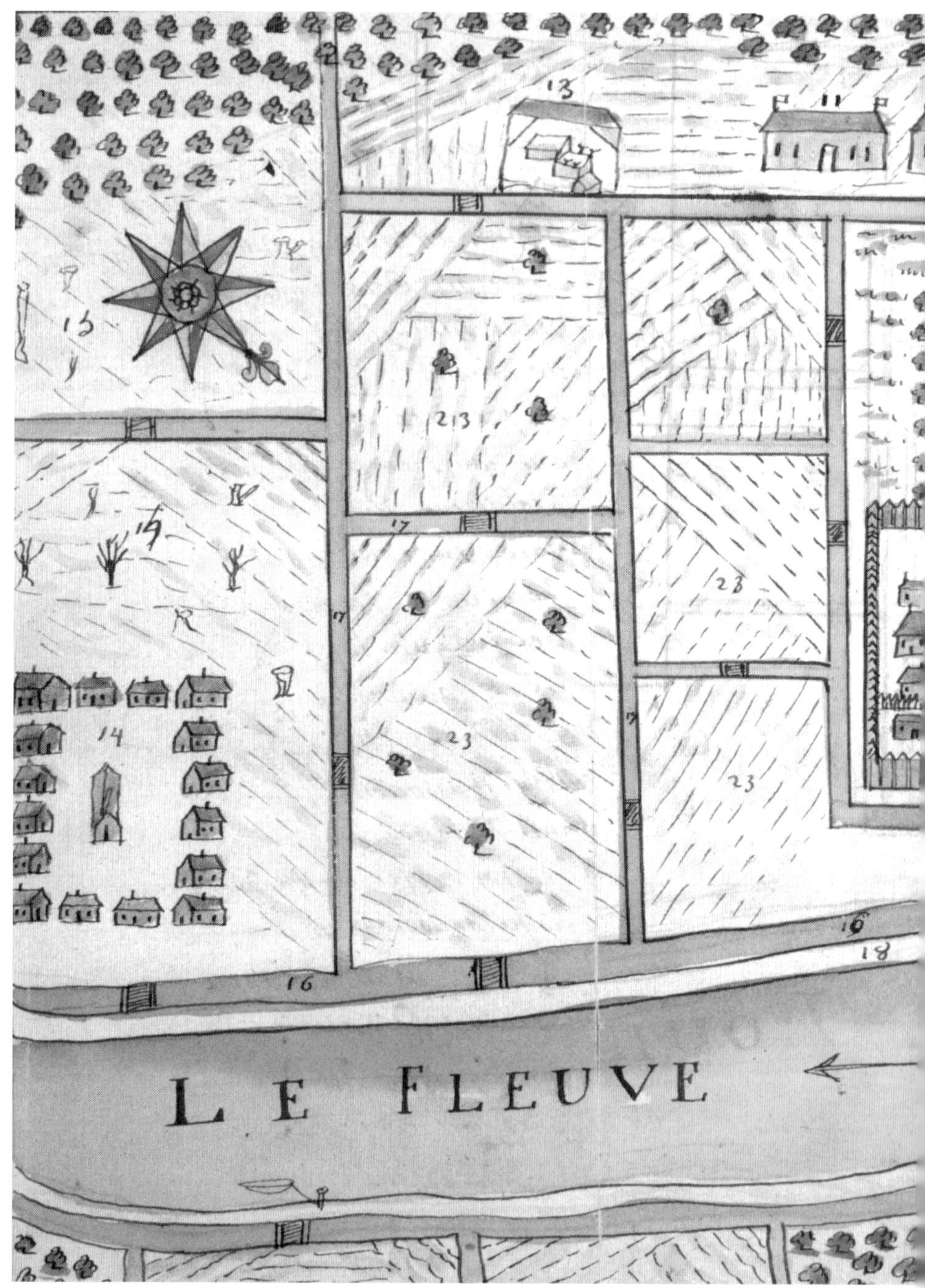
LE FLEUVE

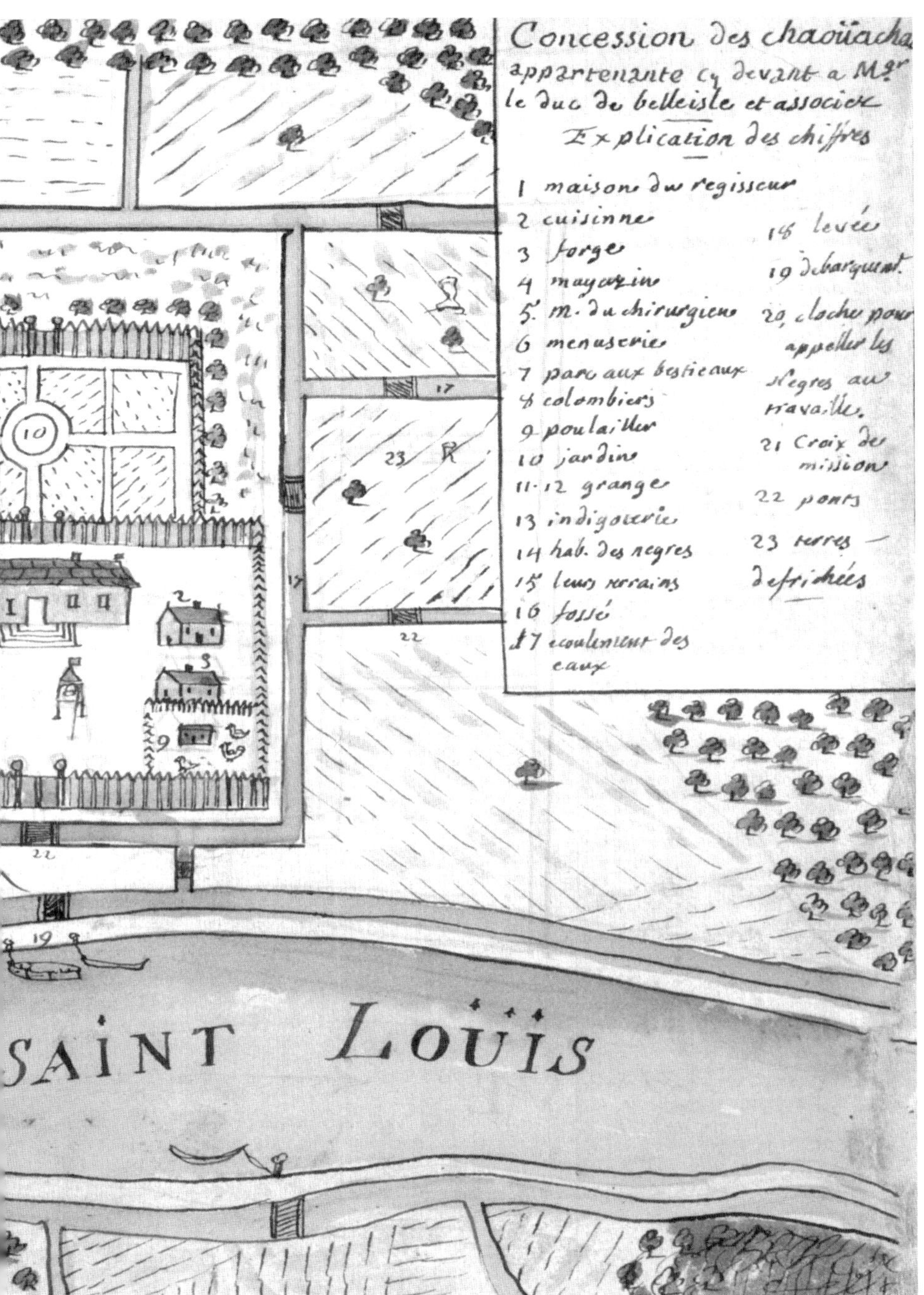

A map at the plantation where the slave Choucoura was subjected to mutilation at the hands of Gaulaz. *Provided by the Norman B. Leventhal Map & Education Center at the Boston Public Library & the ARGO Collection img8.jpg (10).*

Gaulaz took Choucoura back to the concession of Saint Catherine, a landholding in northern Louisiana along the St. Louis River. Upon arriving at the plantation, Gaulaz decided that Choucoura needed to be retrained beyond the normal capabilities of the plantation. Removed from the sight of his fellow enslaved Africans and guarded by the French soldiers on the mission, Gaulaz tied a rope around Choucoura's wrists and then tied him to a post suspended by his wrists. Gaulaz asked Choucoura why he had marooned, and when Choucoura responded that he had fled because Gaulaz was too hard a taskmaster, Gaulaz repeatedly beat Choucoura's head into the post. Gaulaz left the soldiers to guard the enslaved man, and Choucoura dangled from his wrists for several hours. One of the witnesses remarked that Gaulaz was crossing a line, but Gaulaz would hear none of it. The soldiers were disturbed, but they kept their watch. After Choucoura endured hours of agony, Gaulaz returned and untied Choucoura's wrists long enough to shackle him, beating him mercilessly with a cane, and then retied him to the pole. After being left dangling there for several hours, Choucoura's hands were swollen. When he was finally cut down and brought to a surgeon, the surgeon had to remove two fingers from each hand. Though the record says the fingers simply "dropped" from each hand.

Eventually, Choucoura was returned to Sieur de Merveilleux, and in September 1727, de Merveilleux sued Gaulaz for the maltreatment of the slave in his care. From the existence of articles concerning the maltreatment of slaves in the Code Noir of 1724, some students of history walk away with the idea that the French cared for the well-being of the enslaved population, even if only up to a point. However, to consider that any French legal statute was made with concern for the humanity of the enslaved is incorrect. From the beginning, when the courts did investigate the matter, the magistrates

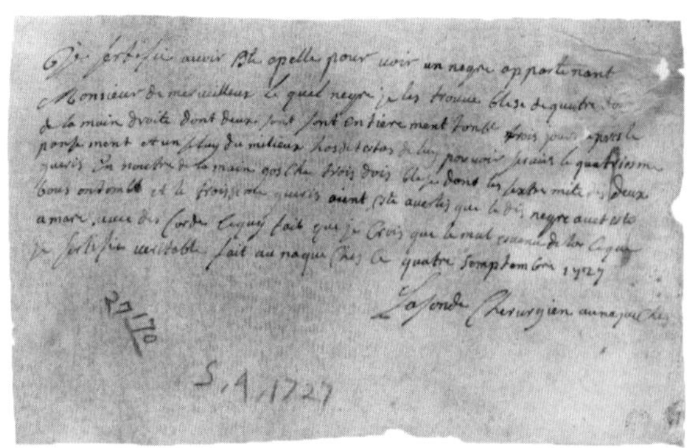

The surgeon Lasonde's report of the gruesome damage done to Choucoura. The enslaved man lost two fingers from one hand and two fingertips from the other. *Provided by the Louisiana Colonial Document Digitization Project # 1727-09-04-02 (09).*

were adjudicating a dispute where a slaveholder's property had been harmed, in this case crippled. At no point did Sieur de Merveilleux want justice for his slave's tarnished honor or mangled sense of human dignity. The Sieur de Merveilleux wanted repayment for the loss of property and profitable labor because of Gaulaz's failure to return the runaway slave safely. Certainly, Gaulaz's blatant abuse of Choucoura made the case easier to prosecute, but restitution was due to Sieur de Merveilleux, not Choucoura. Choucoura had no ability to sue on his own behalf for his own justice.

Beyond legal rights, the Code Noir normalized the maltreatment of people who had been kidnapped, sold or coerced into slavery. In this climate, only the most extreme and public desecration of a slave's legal rights had even the chance of leading to legal trouble for the slaveholder or overseer. And really, this trouble was usually caused by the men employed to coerce the enslaved people on a day-to-day basis. In practice, the Code Noir designated the owners of slaves as victims in the case of an injured slave. From the social station of a plantation owner, they were insulated from all retribution for the maltreatment of slaves. In a legal sense, the plantation owners were not responsible for the actions of their managers, and if an enslaved man was abused by anyone but the plantation owner, then the plantation owner had been wronged, not the slave. So long as the owners of places like the concession of Saint Catherine and slave masters like Sieur de Merveilleux provided the food and clothing set out by the Code Noir to their slaves, they were essentially free from reproach.

Article XIII: Runaways and Slave Gatherings

> *Article XIII. We likewise forbid slaves belonging to different masters to gather by day or by night, under the pretext of a wedding or any other reason, whether on their master's property or elsewhere, and still less in the main roads or the out of the way places, on penalty of corporal punishment, which cannot be less than a whipping and* [branding] *of the fleur de lys; and in case of frequent repetition and other aggravating circumstances, they may be put to death, which we leave to the decision of judges. We require all our subjects to pursue the offenders, and to arrest them, even though there is no order issued against them.*

The story of a pair of runaway slaves named Bontemps and Guillory exemplifies the ways in which the colonial administrators struggled to keep up with the challenges presented by runaway slaves. Throughout the French period of colonization in North America, the inhuman conditions of chattel slavery naturally led enslaved Africans and Native Americans to flee the site of their captivity, usually a plantation field, a small landholding or the galley of a ship. If the slavers allowed the enslaved to flee, then the whole system of slavery would be threatened. So, some of the Code Noir's strictest measures relate to fleeing slaves. In theory, the laws against masters abusing slaves and neglecting their basic needs were also meant to stem the tide of runaways, but in practice the utter desperation of the plantation environment generated most of the crimes committed by slaves.

This is the case with Bontemps and Guillory. Bontemps and Guillory's story ends with the two young enslaved men hanged in public on order of the French court. Bontemps reported himself between eighteen and twenty years of age at the time of his sentencing. His crimes were having fled his master after stealing a small bag of silver coins and then using the coins to buy some brandy. Guillory reported himself as being fifteen years of age at the time of his interrogation. The French court convicted him of having run away twice. For that, Attorney General Fleuriau ordered that Guillory be flogged publicly before being marched to the gallows with Bontemps, where they would both be "hanged and strangled."[36] Usually, the courts and slave owners tended to err on the side of protecting young male slaves. This is because young enslaved Africans and Native Americans were the only people that could be legally forced to labor in the Louisiana wilderness, and the supply chain between West Africa, the French Caribbean and Basse-Louisiane was still nascent and fragile. Bontemps and Guillory were both Native Americans, who were regarded as less desirable by French slavers than enslaved Africans. But that difference in heritage does not explain away the harsh punishment Guillory and Bontemps received. The Code Noir could exact a horrible punishment for Bontemps and Guillory no matter what, but the punishment did not need to represent a loss of investment for the slave owners. But in the case of Bontemps and Guillory, the French courts, necessarily with the consent of the slave owners, promptly executed the two men when there were still other options.

The missing aspect is the fear of runaways being more than individuals. Rather, the French government in New Orleans realized that groups of runaways represented the greatest possible threat to the colonial system. These communities of runaways were called maroons. Bontemps appears to have been connected with some community of runaway slaves. When Councilor Brusle interrogated Bontemps, Bontemps admitted to stealing

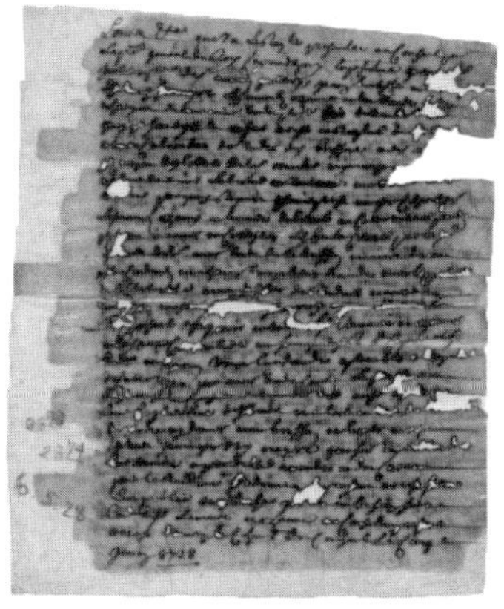

As a result of the investigation into the runaways Guillory and Bontemps, the Superior Council passed this ordinance forbidding the sale of alcohol to slaves. This is an example of how the Superior Council governed by fiat in service to maintaining slavery. *Provided by the Louisiana Colonial Document Digitization Project # 1728-06-05-01 (18).*

his master's silver, running away and using that silver to buy brandy. But when Jean Guillory, the enslaved fifteen-year-old, was interrogated by Brusle on the same day, he confessed that he was tempted to maroon by Bontemps and a cadre of fugitive slaves. With that confession, Guillory set in motion a severe reaction from the French colonial magistrates. Following this confession, the Supreme Council delivered an ordinance forbidding the sale of liquor to slaves without a written order from their owner.[37] Then, the shopkeepers who sold the liquor to slaves were fined twenty livres under the new law.[38] Bontemps and Guillory's initial interrogation occurred on May 31, 1727. The Supreme Council of colonial magistrates published their ordinance on June 5. The bills of information against Guillory and Bontemps were filed a week later. The young men were sentenced to die on June 14, 1727, two weeks after their initial interrogation.

Over the period of French occupation of the Mississippi basin, the colonial controllers developed more sophisticated measures to deal with the problem of runaway slaves and the dangerous societies they built on the fringes of the empire. All the way up to the transfer of the colony to the Spanish, the French were never able to proactively stop enslaved people from deserting the plantations. The rapid flow of enslaved Africans and Native Americans fleeing meant that the French administration had no hope of maintaining functioning records of every instance of marooning. Instead, the colonial records focus on those instances where the regime made real progress or else set and maintained jurisprudence on what to do with enslaved men and women that ran away. Above all, the superior council of the colony and the attorney general, whoever held those positions at a given time, wished to project confidence in the regime's ability to maintain the slaveholding order.

Between 1728, when Guillory and Bontemps ran away, and 1741, the persistence of the runaway slave problem continued to irk the slaveholding class. However, the way the colonial regime responded did not display much finesse or understanding of the problem. In the early decades, the council recorded the instances where an escaped slave was recaptured. But the work of catching escapees fell to bounty hunters and Native American allies. Unless the runaways threatened the regime by congregating or engaging in commerce without the consent of their owners, the superior council seemed to treat marooning as losing one's property. However, in late 1740 and early 1741, the colonial regime began to take a more active interest in policing runaway slaves. The turning point centered on the Chaperon estate. The Chaperon estate lay just outside the fortified perimeter of the original city of New Orleans, what is today known as the French Quarter. It lay on a street called Conde, following a line out from the French Quarter along Chartres Street. Chaperon managed his plantation only a mere four or five miles away from the heart of French colonization in the New World.

Beginning as early as 1736, the Chaperon estate complained to the attorney general, and the rest of the king's representatives, that the issue of runaway slaves was not being dealt with. As we have seen, slave owners were particularly worried when these runaways began to congregate, and by late 1740 the congregations of maroons in the vicinity of the Chaperon estate became intolerable. Residents in the area filed enough complaints that the royal government felt compelled to act. The colonial government tapped Lieutenant Souboye to resolve the issue of the escaped Africans outside of the city. Souboye was a royal official, a member of the king's armed forces, and acted as a representative of the Crown's authority in this matter. Lieutenant Souboye departed for the estate at the head of a contingent made up of free and enslaved Africans.[39] Operating off intelligence gathered from their reports about runaways, Lieutenant Souboye's men tracked down and interrogated a "slave commander" on the Chaperon estate named Pierrot. And according to the report signed by Attorney General Fleuriau on January 10, 1741, the French administrators planned to interrogate Pierrot, discover the "facts" about the escaped Africans Pierrot knew and then promptly put the slave commander on trial.

In colonial Louisiana, the notarized records of the attorney general carried the dual weight of legal record and legal order. Lieutenant Souboye's company detained Pierrot and held him for questioning. Five other enslaved Africans were recovered, and the colonial administration dutifully recorded the name, age and national origin of each enslaved African they captured.[40] The interrogations reveal the increasing interest of the French regime in the logistics of marooning, the bare bones of how runaways survived in the Louisiana wilderness. Pierrot and another slave named Sans Souci both reported surviving in the wetlands outside of New Orleans by trapping small wildlife and squatting in nearby cabins. Escapees of the colony, like Pierrot and Sans Souci, subsisted on a diet of swamp rats and wild cats.[41] However, that fact did not stop Raguet from inquiring of Sans Souci if he knew the whereabouts of some cows and pigs that went missing. Without a doubt, the implication was that Sans Souci and his fellows had stolen the settlers' property to survive.

Further complicating matters was Chaperon himself. The tipping point in the persecution of escaped African slaves might have had little to do with the numbers congregating and more to do with how those escaped slaves were being used by other members of colonial society. In the colonial environment, even those who escaped to the freedom that existed outside the colonial enterprise still had to interact with society at large in order to survive. Pierrot, Sans Souci and the other escapees did not have the means to survive on their own. Trapping swamp rats and living in an abandoned cabin hardly created livable circumstances for the plantation escapees. Rather, judging from the questions that Raguet posed to the captured African slaves, and judging from Monsieur Chaperon's own quick denial of any knowledge of Pierrot's activities in aiding escaped slaves, it is likely that Monsieur Chaperon was employing escaped African slaves as a form of exceedingly cheap labor. Of course, this presented a threat to the entire structure of colonial society.

Usually, French settlers wanted their escaped slaves back in their possession. A petition from November 13, 1730, filed by Madame Marie Barbe-Lionnais shows the fastidious detail that colonists paid to the relative value of their slaves.[42] An exchange of slaves that was perceived by either party as unequal could result in a protracted legal dispute. However, no court records on the sentences given to Pierrot, Sans Souci or the other escapees from near the Chaperon estate have survived. Furthermore, when an enslaved African was put to death, the French administration habitually provided slaveholders with receipts for the value of their slave. But no such receipts for Pierrot, Sans Souci or the other escapees have survived. Given the complications of the case and how the case implicated members of the French colonial elite in benefiting from marooning slaves, it is likely that the captured slaves were either distributed to their previous owners or executed, and thus permanently silenced, for violating the Code Noir.

Article XXVII: Murder and Execution

Either the French colonial regime was less fastidious about their execution records than modern sensibilities would prefer or they were far less likely to execute Europeans and subjects than one might expect. Compared to their treatment of enslaved Africans, which featured regular corporal brutality at the hands of European masters and fellow slaves, Europeans received far more leniency. The Code Noir made it clear that enslaved Africans and Native Americans could be executed for any violence returned to their masters. The principle of greater leniency for the European settlers in matters of violence is an important continuation of the difference in how enslaved and subject received punishment for theft. When we compare the text of the Code Noir with the story of Laborde and the burglary incident at Didier Gaspard's property concerning the enslaved man named Andre:

> *XXVII. The slave who, having struck his master, his mistress, or the husband of his mistress, or their children, shall have produced a bruise, or the shedding of blood in the face, shall suffer capital punishment.*
>
> *XXVIII. With regard to outrages or acts of violence committed by slaves against free persons, it is our will that they be punished with severity, and even with death, should the case require it.*
>
> *XXIX. Thefts of importance, and even the stealing of horses, mares, mules, oxen, or cows, when executed by slaves or manumitted persons, shall make the offender liable to corporal, and even to capital punishment, according to the circumstances of the case.*
>
> *XXX. The stealing of sheep, goats, hogs, poultry, grain, fodder, peas, beans, or other vegetables, produce, or provisions, when committed by slaves, shall be punished according to the circumstances of the case; and the judges may sentence them, if necessary, to be whipped by the public executioner, and branded with the mark of the flower de luce.*[43]

This principle can be found in practice. Comparing the crimes and executions of Kakaracon, an enslaved African executed in 1748, and Degout, a French sculptor executed in 1766, reveals the similarities and differences in the treatment of perpetrators in relation to their race and class. But we can also reinforce the point by looking at the stories we have seen so far. If

Marie Laspronne had been an enslaved African or a free woman of color, those stolen linens would have resulted in her being whipped and branded with the fleur-de-lis. If the runaways from the Chapron estate had been found guilty of stealing any livestock while surviving out in the swamp, they could have been put to death. Being a free person of color did not exempt you from these provisions of the Code Noir.

Throughout the French period, African lives were treated as little more than disposable. The Superior Council usually neglected to update or change any policies toward the enslaved until a problem occurred that affected them. For instance, Raymond D'Ausseville spent decades on the Superior Council in New Orleans and had significant resources in the colony. In 1739, a small boy that D'Ausseville held in bondage was shot by another enslaved boy. All that resulted was D'Ausseville filing an official remonstrance against the practice of allowing enslaved Africans to "handle firearms irresponsibly" and asking for the white overseer in the case to be held liable.[44] D'Ausseville was worried only about how he was going to cover the loss of a laboring soul. Generally, the society of colonial Louisiana placed very little value on the lives of slaves outside of their capacity to labor. The deaths of enslaved Africans mattered to the judges only if they needed to be arbitrated for value owed or if the enslaved had crossed the ultimate taboo and assaulted a European.

Kakaracon "Charlot," owned by Jean Baptiste Raguet, crossed that line. The case of Charlot offers insight into how seriously the French magistrates took violations of Article XXVIII of the Code Noir. What exactly happened to Kakaracon in the woods in early January 1748 will never be known. However, the Superior Council spent an unusual amount of effort finding the facts of the case. Their efforts over a two-week period included interrogating a dozen enslaved Africans, long and tedious confrontations, and detaining four slaves for the duration of the investigation. From the court records and interrogations, all translated by the Louisiana Historical Society, a clearer story emerges.

In January 1748, a French soldier named Bon Envie went hunting on property nearby the barracks. The slaves who lived on the property sometimes set out traps to supplement their diet, and one slave in particular, named Kakaracon, spent much of his free time trapping birds, wild cats and other small game. If Kakaracon's notarized confession from the day of his execution is truthful, then he and one other accomplice, Pierrot, held down the French soldier and stabbed him in the stomach.[45] There is no doubt that someone stabbed Bon Envie. He was found moaning in a field and rushed to a doctor by three slaves, all of whom were interrogated when the soldier died. Kakaracon, having been seen wearing a bloody shirt and carrying a knife, was arrested and interrogated. Other slaves who knew Kakaracon offered that he had a bad disposition, and a few of them even claimed that the murder weapon was the same weapon as Kakaracon's knife, that the knife belonged to Kakaracon. The other slaves did not like Kakaracon, and none of them confirmed his alibis, no matter how hard he tried to combine the stories during interrogation.

Kakaracon pleaded that he hunted the woods, what the records refer to as the plantation's "desert," regularly and that the blood on his clothes and wounds on his hands came from the wild game he hunted. It made some sense. An enslaved man could not carry around a weapon, particularly a firearm, without his master's permission. The traps that Kakaracon left for the animals likely only wounded the larger ones. The knife could also be used to dress the meat and prepare it to be taken back to the plantation. Perhaps Kakaracon's familiarity with the woodlands only deepened his accuser's suspicions—familiarity with hunting the woods could look like a motive to protect the woods from competition. The investigators reasoned that Kakaracon or any other slaves would have a vested interest in protecting an important source of meat. The accused worked splitting wood at the plantation—endless days of manual labor could drive a man well past his limit with hunger and desperation. January is the height of winter, and while Louisiana winters are relatively mild and wet, fresh shipments of grain were not coming in from Europe any time soon. Hunger is central to the story. One of Kakaracon's alibis, the one he stuck to the longest, was that he was roasting potatoes with a friend and eating rice with other slaves. Men like Kakaracon had to eat in order to survive the day's labor. Men like Bon Envie must have wanted to taste anything except another ration of gunner's bread. That those two men, encountering each other in the woods, would fight rather than go through another day of hunger seemed reasonable.

With Laborde and Pontuel, the Superior Council seemed to have dropped the matter entirely. But Kakaracon was accused of killing a white man and a soldier. His actions threatened the order of the colony, and he was governed by the Code Noir. Kakaracon was sentenced to be marched through town holding a torch, led to a large wooden wheel and then broken upon the wheel, his body and limbs shattered. If that did not kill him, the Superior Council ordered in secret to have him strangled afterward. Kakaracon carried the entire act on his shoulders. Every other slave arrested in connection with the murder of Pierre Olivy, known as Bon

Envie, was interrogated and then sent back to their owners. The plantation owners were allowed to punish their slaves as they wished. Before his deathbed confessions on the morning of his execution, the last piece of attention the Superior Council paid to Kakaracon was to furnish Raguet, his owner, with a receipt. The receipt valued Kakaracon at 1,300 livres. There is no further description of the day of Kakaracon's execution. He was likely brought to the center of town and affixed to a large spoked wheel. The wheel was turned to break his limbs, and after exposure and further torture, Kakaracon was likely strangled to death.

One reason that this case received so much attention is likely because Jean Baptiste Raguet not only owned a small plantation outside of the city but also served as the official notary for the Superior Council. Raguet's name is scattered across decades of colonial records. Jean Baptiste was no small white citizen. And his slave had murdered a soldier of the French kingdom over some hunting game. He stood to lose quite a lot if the case did not go correctly. Under the Code Noir:

> *XXXI. In cases of thefts committed or damages done by their slaves, masters, besides the corporal punishment inflicted on their slaves, shall be bound to make amends for the injuries resulting from the acts of said slaves, unless they prefer abandoning them to the sufferer. They shall be bound so to make their choice, in three days from the time of the conviction of the negroes; if not, this privilege shall be forever forfeited.*

This meant that if Kakaracon had implicated Raguet in some way, or if Raguet had tried to defend his slave against the charges, Raguet would have been liable for the death of a soldier. So, no matter what, Kakaracon had to be executed with a story that washed Raguet's hands of any wrongdoing in the scenario. And in that scenario, the Code Noir laid out some helpful protections for men like Raguet:

> *XXXVI. The slave who is sentenced to suffer death on the denunciation of his master, shall, when that master is not an accomplice to his crime, be appraised before his execution by two of the principal inhabitants of the locality, who shall be especially appointed by the judge, and the amount of said appraisement shall be paid to the master. To raise this sum, a proportional tax shall be laid on every slave, and shall be collected by the persons invested with that authority.*

> *XXXVII. We forbid all the officers of the Superior Council, and all our other officers of justice in this colony, to take any fees or receive any perquisites in criminal suits against slaves, under the penalty, in so doing, of being dealt with as guilty of extortion.*[46]

It seems questionable whether or not Raguet served as an officer of justice. Given that he collected the receipt of Kakaracon's value, it seems at least possible that Jean Baptiste received a reimbursement from the state for the whole affair.

Conclusions

As modern Americans, we have an inherent sense that a judicial system is meant to do right and that the court is meant to mete out justice. We make a fatal mistake by letting this modern sense of a court color our understanding of early modern pre-revolutionary courts. Early modern courts existed to resolve the disputes between property holders, whether it be a lord with a vast estate or a merchant farmer whose property included wife, children, and slaves. Courts developed in Europe to negotiate important topics between property holders. They did not develop to uphold the rights of slaves. Courts never considered treating each man equally before the law. What if one man was nobility and the other a serf? For early modern France, the law clearly stated that the nobleman won out over the serf. When the children of continental lords and middle-class merchants raising their heads for the first time struck out across the Atlantic, wealth and power on their mind, the courts they brought with them mirrored those back in Europe. They became the undisputed authorities in their new territories. The small whites served as a stand in for the city artisans and landed peasantry. Plantation owners spread the enslaved Africans thick across the bottom of the colonial hierarchy and abused their station as much as possible for profit. The plantation owners did not invent using courts to uphold their power. That trick had come around long ago, and they were just the most able practitioners in the New World.

So when enslaved Africans were subjected to the Code Noir by the slaveholders who had a hand in writing it—remember that Bienville returned to Paris to consult on the 1724 Code Noir—those enslaved Africans were not brought up on clear charges in front of an impartial judge seeking justice. Tracing the history of the Code's enforcement is tricky because the French courts enforced it like a moeur, a way that things *already were* and thus *had to be.* They did not often go in front of a judge and claim that such-and-such enslaved person broke a given statute of the Code Noir. It would be a fascinating project to go through each statute of the Code Noir and look for evidence of its enforcement. But the reality is that the Code Noir served as a crude and clever cudgel for colonial jurists to keep African slaves in line. The sheer violence is its crude nature. The Code Noir is blatantly supported by nothing but the whip and execution. But its cleverness comes from how it served to subject African slaves perpetually while also providing for the protection of the enslaved as *property*. This was no protection for the enslaved. The plantation owners had a legal protection of their enslaved property so that members of the small-white class could not abuse their valuable sources of labor—but that is the extent of the Code's protections for African slaves.

One of the French Revolution's remarkable effects was proving that the French government could legislate against slavery. Such a simple goal remained unfeasible until the French Revolution of 1789 paved the way for extensive reforms of the French kingdom. Those laws did not last very long, and the revolutionaries were too busy among themselves to truly abolish the practice. Napoleon, who fought the kings of Europe through to Moscow's door and supposedly spread a nationalist virtue across Europe, reintroduced slavery into the French colonies in 1802, and the institution remained legal until the end of the 1840s. After Napoleon was defeated and exiled by the revenging monarchs of Europe, the Code Noir continued to exist as a set of customs that informed the regulation of slavery—the exact opposite of what the much-touted Napoleonic Code promised French subjects. The two seem to have existed side by side in perfect paradoxical equilibrium. Slavery became unfashionable during the July Monarchy and the Code Noir along with it. The French regime made some efforts to change how slaveholders treated the enslaved Africans in their midst. Ultimately, only the Revolution of 1848 set up the final abolition of slavery within the French empire and the final death of the Code Noir along with it. By the time the second French Republic abolished slavery, the former Louisiana territory made up a vast part of the western United States,[47] and slavery would not be abolished there until Abraham Lincoln's Emancipation Proclamation in 1863. When Napoleon sold Louisiana, its resources and the people living there to the Americans in the largest real estate deal in modern history, entrance into the Union ensured that those enslaved in the former Louisiana territory remained enslaved for fifteen years longer than slaves in the French empire.

In classic French imperial fashion, the governments involved in the Louisiana Purchase had to commit to two flag-raising ceremonies because they failed to consider the weather and had failed to mark the transfer of power from 1800.[48] In the Treaty of San Ildefonso, the French obtained the Louisiana territory from the Spanish after losing it to the Spanish in 1762. The French and the Americans finalized the Louisiana Purchase in April 1803, a scarce few years after acquiring the territory. In November 1803, the residents of New Orleans found out they were to be Americans in thirty days—a fact announced at a long-delayed ceremony that placed the French flag atop the pole in the *place d'armes.* The crowd was reportedly angry at the turn of events. In New Orleans, delays meant that the ceremony intended to mark the annexation by the United States did not occur until December—when it was too cold for those north of New Orleans to even hear the news. St. Louis needed their own ceremony. The St. Louis ceremony finally took place in 1804. The day of the ceremony became known as Three Flag Day because the French and Spanish administrators had never held a proper transfer ceremony. The St. Louis residents felt like it was proper to transfer first from the Spanish to the French flag, throw themselves a wild party and then greet the American flag with the morning's hangover. It may be the only time St. Louis has thrown a better party than New Orleans, which is no mean feat. But it also shows how the residents of the Louisiana territory were steeped in an Old World, colonial mentality up to the moment of their annexation by the United States. The old flags of Europe and the old European codes still held weight in Louisiana. The citizens of St. Louis reportedly could not contain their enthusiasm for being French citizens again. The citizens of New Orleans did not enjoy the bait-and-switch routine between France and the United States.

The change from Spanish and French rule to American rule created an opportunity for the ghost of the Code Noir to survive until emancipation. The U.S. federal government left most of the regulation of slavery to the states. When the new legislature convened in 1806, they created a new set of laws to govern the established parishes of the "Orleans Territory." Within Orleans Territory, the territorial legislature created a system of laws to govern the newly admitted territory. Of course, educated men who felt the need to publish their new legal codes in English and French created a legal system that suited their era and interests. The 1806 Black Code removed some of the bloodthirsty punishments from the 1724 edition of the Code, and it retained some of the lessons from the previous century of plantation slavery. Section 24 of the 1806 Black Code reaffirmed the 1727 ordinance prohibiting the sale of liquor to slaves. The new Code also relieved slave masters from almost any complicity in any wrongdoing of their slaves. No matter whether a slave was caught riding a horse, carrying goods without a written note or traveling with a weapon of any kind, if the slave master disavowed the slave, they were relieved of nearly all repercussions. Of course, Black codes continued to govern African Americans after the end of slavery and through the era of segregation, but with the end of legal slavery in the whole of the former Louisiana territory, an era of explicit abuse, dehumanization and destruction came to an end.

3

CIVIL MATTERS AND COLONIAL GOVERNMENT

All that was European did not simply dissipate into the murky expanse of Louisiana. Through force of arms and by the fiat of kingly power, the French kingdom planted a judiciary within the colony that occupied an important space within colonial society. The New World's judiciary existed to negotiate the terms of social cohabitation. Or, to put it another way, the French courts had the very important job of ensuring that some sort of rules governed how French settlers interacted. Every bit of evidence suggested that if there were no rules, things would quickly dissolve into strings of larceny and murder up and down the bayou. Everyone came to the New World with their own ideas of "the law" in their heads. The courts existed to reconcile the differences and ensure that the king's law remained as steadfast as it was in Europe. These settlers, or the white, propertied, male and French settlers who mattered in the French legal code, all participated in the courts. The courts arbitrated their disputes, and the settlers even abided by the court's rulings. At times, this judiciary would attempt to lean on the old way of doing things and thus shape the colony in the image of Europe. And at other moments, the propertied men of Louisiana would have to forge their own path. The French Superior Court became the main, and sometimes only, institution that served this function within the entire Louisiana territory, not just the Basse-Louisiane region. Indeed, the men of the colony would facilitate resolutions to disputes between trades as far north as Illinois territory.

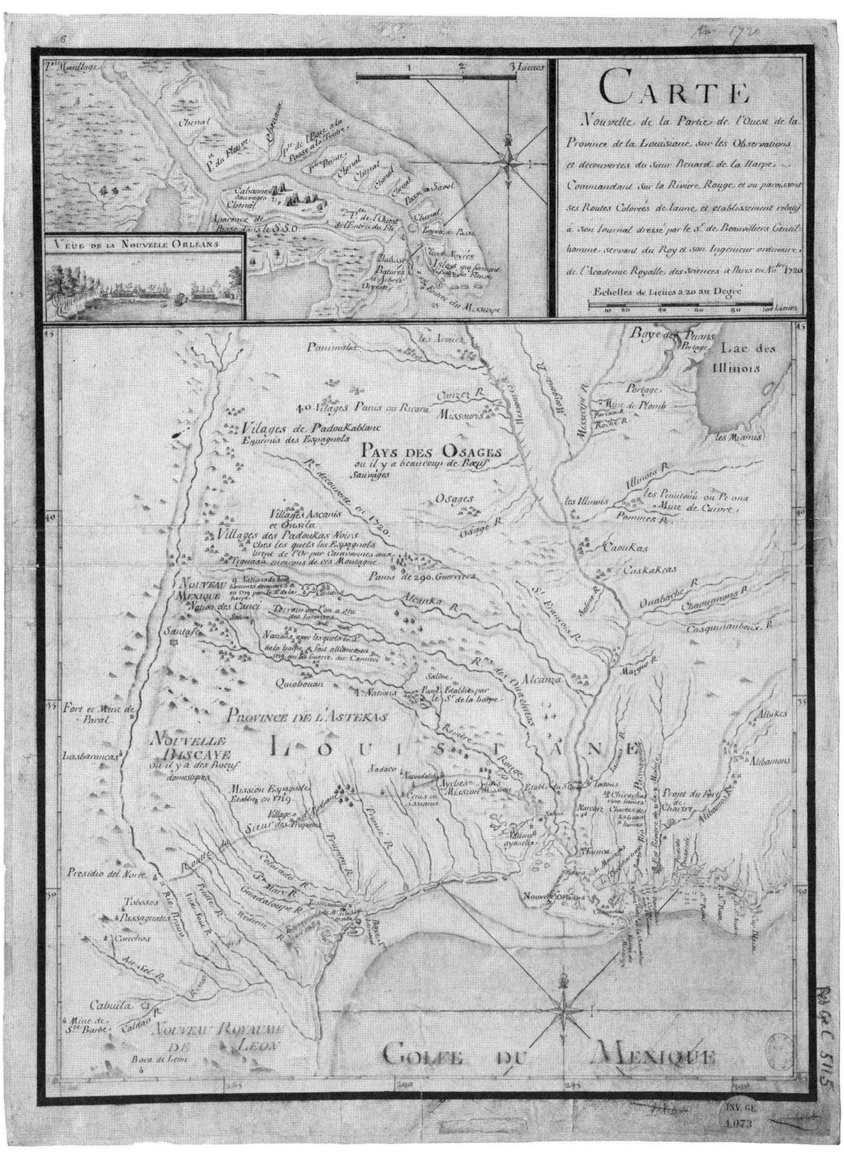

An early map of Louisiana produced by and for the Company of the West. The small depiction of New Orleans and the larger map are presented in full here. This map helps visualize what the French understood to be the land under their administration. *Retrieved from the Library of Congress Digital Collection img13.jpg (33).*

The French Superior Court was a council composed of the leading propertied Frenchmen of the colony and headed by the attorney-general of the colony. The counciliar aspect of the court is particularly French and reflects the *parlements* of the age in the French kingdom. These propertied men spent a significant amount of time devoted to the management of the colony. They were not the upper-middle-class and meritocratic politicians of the later United States. Rather, these were men with an Old World sense of justice that favored a cultivated sense of disinterest. Back on the continent, the men who governed other men were not supposed to dirty themselves in the affairs of trade and business, and their business was to manage their slice of the kingdom. The men of the French Superior Court straddled that line. No perfectly landed French aristocrat without an itch for adventure bothering his soul set out for the Louisiana territory. The men of the French Superior Court, along with all the men in the Louisiana territory, wanted to be that rich someday. The Louisiana territory is how the men of the Superior Court, along with the attorneys generals and governors, intended to garner their riches.

It was this intent to gather riches that caused the greatest amount of discord within French Louisiana. While the other French islands were relatively profitable and did produce new wealth for the French upper classes, the Louisiana territory registered a loss on the king's books year after year. Hopes of finding silver in the Illinois country never manifested anything more than some lead mines. These lead mines spurred what little development the Missouri River basin saw from the French, but no riches ever flowed down from the interior of the continent. In an age where empires focused their economic programs on the hoarding of precious metals within their kingdoms, the vast Louisiana territory offered almost nothing to the French economy. For the French kingdom, the economic reality proved disastrous. The utter poverty of French Louisiana bedeviled Antoine Crozat, drove John Law into the ground and sent governors like Vaudrieul into a panic at least once during their terms. So it was that the men with nearly unlimited magisterial power, the French Superior Council, were also the men with a vested interest in a permanently failing enterprise.

In order to understand the divide between rich and poor, it helps to borrow the class distinctions that formed in Haiti among the white settlers. In Haiti, the settlers divided into the classes of "big whites" and "small whites" as land became scarcer in the colony and the plantations were monopolized. The big whites owned land and slaves. They could produce enough cash crops to sell, and eventually they could escape the colony and return to

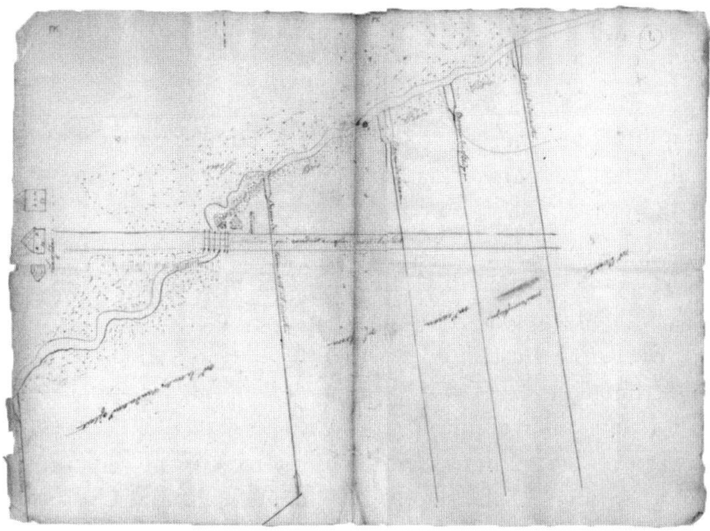

A good map of a plantation estate and its landmarks from just after the French period of colonial Louisiana. This serves as a fine example of the layout of a French plantation as the French colonists perceived it. *Provided by the Louisiana Colonial Document Digitization Project # 1780-04-19-01.1 (22 23).*

France to live in luxury off the profits. The small whites (petit blancs) were those white colonists who either did not have any land or property or had comparatively little. In the Louisiana colony, the big whites had an absolute monopoly on the courts. If a dispute went in front of the Superior Council and there was a clear class distinction, the big white usually received the favorable ruling. Bienville himself benefited from this when a squatter began to improve on some of the governor's land. The would-be homesteader pleaded his case, but the Superior Council voted for his eviction from the premises and a small cash reimbursement for his trouble.[49]

The plethora of civil matters that busied the Superior Council's daily docket flowed from two particular economic ailments that hampered the colony's development. The first economic problem was the inflation crisis that struck French paper bills in the eighteenth century, in particular the Louisiana Company bills and the royal paper livres. No French colonial currency was able to retain its value for very long, and colonists far preferred specie coins to paper money. The second economic problem stemmed from the administration's heavy reliance on monopolies to control the resource wealth of the Louisiana territory. This extended beyond the Gulf Coast and deep into Illinois territory. The practice of monopolization in the eighteenth century extended above the colonial administrators, too. Bienville, Vaudrieul and the other governors all operated in a world where the king of France personally owned all of the Mississippi River basin and leased the rights of exploitation out either to major international corporations like John Law's Louisiana Company or multiple closely selected Frenchmen to exploit smaller and more remote resources.

In some cases, social tensions made suffering the economic conditions unbearable. At every juncture, the subjects confined to the Louisiana territory remained trapped in a world that could rule on nearly any topic by administrative fiat. Successions, the care of children, ruling on the rights of squatters, settling land and labor disputes, distributing monopolies, resolving wills, the care of orphan children, enforcing the upkeep of the commons and every other possible civil matter ended up in front of the Superior Council. Over time, the rulings of the Superior Council meant that white settlers and Black slaves were separated, that poor whites were forced into unprofitable and dangerous professions and dissenters were crushed with an unyielding fist. Mostly, the Superior Council settled disputes over successions, tried to collect money from merchants skipping town and registered, or sometimes decided, who owned a piece of land.

Interjecting themselves across the neat social hierarchy of colonial Louisiana were two other classes: soldiers and merchants. These classes disrupted the finest dreams for an orderly colony of the administrators and aristocrats. Always a merchant was skipping town while owing thousands of livres, getting murdered by Native Americans halfway up the Mississippi River or plotting some smuggling scheme to the nearby Spanish colonies of Pensacola and Cuba.[50] However, the merchants were indispensable. They held the contracts to leave the French kingdom's ports of call, and they imported the enslaved Africans to the Gulf South. At the end of the day, unless a silver mine materialized in Illinois and solved the kingdom's economic troubles, the colony was there to be exploited by the merchant-frontiersmen. Merchants were a troublesome lifeblood.

The soldiers, on the other hand, rarely made too much commotion. But when they did, it often prompted fast action from the royal governor or the Superior Council. Soldiers existed to enforce order in the colony on behalf of the king—at least, the orderly profit of the king's men in the colony. But they also served as a police force within the colony, armed auxiliaries for any adventures into the frontier and brutal slave catchers. Soldiers cared more about their relative comfort and the readiness of supplies more than anything else. It takes a rare case of cruelty, buffoonery or both to make a colonial soldier question his orders. But occasionally, soldiers did question orders—and the Superior Council treated mutineers to the gallows rope.

As different as the merchant and soldier classes were, they shared a critical flashpoint. Both the merchants and the soldiers of the Louisiana territory suffered under the scarcity of bread. Bread was an essential flashpoint in a number of cases in the middle of the eighteenth century, not the least of which was the Bad Bread Mutiny. A petition from July 30, 1745, the same year as the Bad Bread Mutiny, showed that merchants were not being reimbursed for the price of the bread that was going to the soldiers. The colonial regime simply took the grain and forgot about the bill. The precarious nature of life in Louisiana, especially in the first half of the eighteenth century, meant that propertied individuals had to resort to the Superior Council for relief when things went wrong, even if the agents of the Superior Council, or their fellows, were the ones wronging them.

How the Governors Ran the Colony

The Louisiana colony needed to make money for the French Crown. The Crown did not want to manage the colony itself, so the French court contracted men like Antoine Crozat and John Law to manage the colony for them. But Crozat and Law were both financiers, not adventurers, explorers or plantation managers. They did not want to get close to the dirty business of the Louisiana colony. Antoine Crozat and John Law never visited Louisiana. Both men hired managers to make any land they owned productive. And they did not want to handle the daily, or even weekly, affairs of the colony. In order to fill these administrative positions, men like John Law and Antoine Crozat selected governors that represented the king in civil and military matters within the colony. These governors came from a small cadre of minor nobility and landed gentry that had a shared background of diplomacy, familiarity with the New World and some naval experience. As Governors Vaudreuil and Bienville both learned during their careers, if you had the right experience and stood in the right room in Versailles at the right time, it was not difficult to seize control of Louisiana. The official name of this position was the "royal governor," but men like Bienville would serve as interim governors for long stretches of time. But more than anything else, a royal governor's career turned on the ability of the governor to manage the colony's internal affairs while also keeping the chattering advisors in Versailles at bay.

Unfortunately for the governors, they also had their own cadre of chattering advisors that often worked against them. These men were the financial controllers, the members of the Superior Council, the lieutenant generals of the colony and anyone else that the Crown gave a mandate to oversee some section. Living in a world ruled by absolute fiat meant that the chain of command could become quickly snared at any level lower than the king's. No governor was more famous for constantly fighting and creating rivalries than Bienville. And Bienville did not argue with anyone as much as the colony's accountants. Many of the governors attempted to run clean and efficient administrations, but most of the governors of Louisiana that history remembers as "great" are the military men who allowed smuggling across imperial lines and diplomacy with the Native Americans. Bienville's rapport with the Native Americans reached legendary stature by the end of his tenure. Bienville managed to pivot his meager resources and inferior bargaining position, compared to the British especially, into generational loyalties with the Native Americans. Bienville's successors messed up the situation with the Native Americans, and his reputation grew by contrast.

The power of the governors of New France looked different than the powers of governors today. None of these men were popularly elected. Bienville was the third governor of Louisiana, and the only two before him were short stints by his elder brother, Iberville, and a close comrade of the two named de Sauvole. And this is a technicality, too. For the first part of his career as New France's primary administrator, Bienville held the lesser military title of comandante. From when Bienville was dismissed from his post the first time in 1713 to when he died in Paris, each new governor appointed to the position seemed to be chosen to lessen Bienville's power over the colony. Each of them would ultimately find ruin in Louisiana without Bienville's aid. Cadillac, l'Epinay and Perier all found themselves on the outside of Bienville's circle of influence, and none of them seemed to last very long. None of them outlasted Bienville's career in New France. Bienville's first true successor, Vaudreuil, embraced and improved on the Bienville model of governance. Especially after deviating from Bienville's policies led to the Natchez Massacre, governors did what they could to keep the Native Americans as happy as Bienville had done.

In the broadest sense, the governors controlled the colony because the king said it was so, and the soldiers followed the representative of the king. In practice, New France's power was increasingly diffused the farther one wandered from the Superior Council. The magistrates had incredible power over property rights, acquisitions, trade and interpreting legal codes. Men like Jean-Baptiste Raguet, an official notary of the empire, could request troop deployments with a simple petition and a persuasive argument. The Superior Council could order those deployments. The governor was far from a military dictator. Instead, the governor most often dealt with the France-facing side of administration, dealing with the courtiers in Versailles and attempting to manage the distribution of land among them. These distributions were called concessions. The governor's job entailed creating concessions for potential investors out of the surveyed land. Investors that could bring hundreds of people received large allotments of land outside of New Orleans. Bienville, and every governor that wanted to last long enough in their position to make any money, made sure to grant themselves some prime land. They used their power over land to make powerful friends among the plantation elite, and they used their connections with the courtiers in France to control the merchants within the settlements.

Bienville's reputation for corruption led to accusations of despotism. More than anything else, Louis XIV and his advisors could not stand an upstart. But no one else seemed capable of doing the job. The first replacement for Bienville, Cadillac, turned out to be an even bigger fraud than Bienville, or maybe just unlucky. Within three years of Cadillac's appointment, Antoine Crozat had grown so exhausted of Bienville and Cadillac's bickering that he resigned administering the colony for the kingdom. Cadillac's earlier misadventures in Detroit compounded with his failures in New France landed him in the Bastille, though he died in a cozy position in Castel-Sarrasin. It seemed that Louisiana needed a leader who could manage the affairs of the people within the colony, who could grease the wheels without upsetting the cart. But he always came back with a slightly different view on administration. He learned from his competitors.

The control that governors had over the colony came from land and weapons, but their superiors marked a governor's success by how profitable that land was. For this reason, and for the reason of the plantation owners seeking profit themselves, governors of Louisiana became integral to the introduction of the slave trade. Bienville spent months ensuring that the first slaves would be brought to Louisiana plantations, where they could begin doing the backbreaking labor settlement required. Bienville also advised on the authorship of the Code Noir and paid careful attention to how Caribbean slavers managed their vast fields. Bienville's truest successor, Vaudreuil, introduced the sugarcane industry into Louisiana. Between the two of them, no other single institution did more for the introduction of slavery than the governorship of Louisiana. The other governors sought to manage the affairs of the colony as best they could while advancing each of their individual interests.

This pattern held true throughout the period of French control. Only the world-shaking events of the French and Indian War, in Europe called the Seven Years' War, could shake the pattern of French dominion over Louisiana. After the embarrassing end of the Seven Years' War, the French lost most of their North American holdings. The French dream of a trans-Atlantic empire that dominated two continents, Europe and North America, died with the end of the war. Only Napoleon would attempt to briefly resurrect that dream, and the Haitians would put an end to it once and for all. Despite the adversity created by cross-continental conflict, the French governors of Louisiana stayed with the colony through to the bitter end. Even after the French had technically lost control of the colony after the events of the Seven Years' War, the French governors still managed the territory. A revolt in 1768 that threw out the first Spanish governor of Louisiana, Governor Ulloa, brought the conflict between settlers, colonial elites and European aristocrats to a head. The 1768 Louisiana Revolt also showed that the divisions between classes, which the French empire had purposefully created, had grown so large as to be unworkable across a large empire.

The final French governor of the colony of Louisiana, Charles Phillipe Aubry, encapsulated the feelings of betrayal, loss and sheer greed that defined the waning days of French rule. Charles Phillipe Aubry became embroiled as a central figure in the 1768 revolt against Spanish rule. Aubry was the governor of Louisiana when his Spanish replacement, Ulloa, arrived in the colony. Aubry handed over control of the colony to the Spanish representatives, as was demanded by his French superiors and the French-signed Treaty of Fontainebleau. But when Ulloa took over, the powerful French planters who had long ago laid their roots in Louisiana would have nothing to do with Spanish rule. These French planters were Creoles, those born in the colonies and not in mainland Europe. They were also men of wealth and means whom other colonists relied on for food, supplies, jobs and social stability. Most important to these men of means and their small white colonial comrades were the goods and supplies that came into the colony illegally—that is to say, smuggled goods that were cheaper because the merchant did not have to pay exorbitant shipping taxes. These goods made life in the colony viable and sometimes even pleasurable. And Governor Ulloa intended to tame the port of New Orleans and implement harsh Spanish trade laws.

Governor Aubry was a man who wanted to serve the French empire. He had been a soldier in the French and Indian War and served with distinguished honors in the Canadian theater. Among his peers, Aubry had a reputation for bravery in the field, but in Louisiana histories, the events of 1768 would forever doom Aubry to accusations of cowardice and betrayal. Neither Ulloa nor Aubry had many troops at their disposal, and Ulloa's plans to enforce the colony's port laws had alienated both men from the rich Creole planters that controlled institutions like the Superior Council. Under the impression that the transfer of Louisiana between France and Spain had become confused, and realizing that they did not want to serve a Spanish king or a Spanish empire, the Creole elite, Acadian refugees and German settlers launched a revolt against Aubry and Ulloa. The day of the revolt, Aubry went in front of the Superior Council, which had become the institution closest to leading the French revolt against Spanish rule, and attempted to persuade them against their course of action. When he failed, the Superior Council took charge of the colony and eventually forced Governor Ulloa out of the colony—but not before Aubry had to put his life on the line and defend Ulloa against the upstart colonists.

Eventually, Aubry became the only voice of reason left in a colony run by a Superior Council gone mad. Months passed before the second Spanish governor of Louisiana, Governor O'Reilly, arrived. Understanding that Louisiana now posed a military problem that demanded a military solution, the new governor arrived with a flotilla in order to subdue the colony. Aubry helped calm the people of New Orleans and keep them in good order. When O'Reilly arrived, he summoned the interim governor for his report. Aubry's true loyalties became infamous. When O'Reilly summoned Aubry for his report on the situation, Aubry told O'Reilly precisely whom the conspirators were that stole the colony from the Spanish Crown, and the men, including the colony's beloved revolutionary Lafreniere, were executed. In the end, all that was left for Aubry to do was leave the colony a tattered mess—but a Spanish mess, not a French one. Rumors have dogged Aubry through the centuries that he absconded with stolen treasure, but these rumors are likely false. The man knew to expect a fine pension from the crown upon his return. But the seas had other plans. On the way back to France, a storm swept across the *Pere de Famille* and sank the ship, killing all but a handful of passengers.

Governor Vaudreuil, the Money Crisis and Monopolies

Of all of the governors that attempted to squeeze something desirable out of the Louisiana territory, not the least of which was Bienville himself, Governor Vaudreuil stands out as the one French governor of Louisiana that understood how to complete the mission. Pierre de Rigaud de Vaudreuil de Cavagnial, Marquis de Vaudreuil, spent a ten-year term as the governor of French Louisiana followed by an ignoble stint as the last governor-general of New France during the Seven Years' War. His career occurred during one of the most interesting times in French colonial history. Vaudreuil's tenure occurred after Bienville's tenure ended, in the period when French influence among the Native Americans waned, English influence continued to spread across the continent and an inflation crisis ate away at the core of the colonial economy. When Vaudreuil received his appointment in 1743, the colony's crisis had not yet become an existential threat. By 1763, the British and the Spanish controlled all of New France and had obliterated the French colonial regime. So, Vaudreuil was at once the man best suited to the job of being the governor of Louisiana and the man who would let the whole of New France slip through his fingers.

Who was Governor Rigaud de Vaudreuil, and what gave him the right to such a tragic fate? Governor Vaudreuil was the descendent of provincial nobility turned into noble frontier-soldiers in service of the king. The Vaudreuil dynasty had been outflanked in the power and prestige politics of the late middle ages. For a provincial noble family, French Canada represented an opportunity to curry favor with the royal court and steal some prestige for the dynasty. Rigaud de Vaudreuil's father, Phillipe de Vaudreuil, relocated to French Canada for that reason. Phillipe was the youngest son not enrolled in the Church and thus joined the prestigious musketeer corps as a young man. Phillipe de Vaudreuil made a name for himself as a competent, steadfast commanding officer. The musketeer corps also carried the extra boon of serving the king of France directly, and so the young Phillipe was able to begin gaining notoriety in Versailles.

Phillipe de Vaudreuil's ambitions drove him to become the governor of Montreal and the governor-general of New France in turn. No less than Louis XIV appointed him to his governorships, and during the elder Vaudreuil's tenure his power over the colonies was nearly uncontested—though nowhere near absolute. But for Louis XIV and the French kingdom, having a leader whose social connections were rooted in the area he administered turned out to be a decisive advantage. Vaudreuil paid particular attention to the health of the fur trade and the strength of New France's relations with the Native American tribes along the northern frontier. He witnessed firsthand how the War of Spanish Succession bankrupted the empire and alienated New France from its Native American allies. The normal state of affairs between New France and the English colonies was violent tension. For this reason, Phillipe de Vaudreuil always paid close attention to the English colonies and never let them live peacefully for too long. Phillipe de Vaudreuil even influenced the removal of Antoine de Cadillac from his Detroit post, which began de Cadillac's long string of misadventures in the Louisiana and Illinois territories.

After the Sun King died, he left behind a modern, deadly and bankrupt empire. The court of Louis XV was left to pick up after the party, and they were perfectly content to allow the children of the first generation of French colonial administrators to fight over the titles their fathers and uncles once claimed. This system worked well for Versailles. The children of nobility would come to them and compete for royal favor in hopes of being *appointed* to a position of responsibility. Soldiering governors did not retire to landed estates supported by peasants bound to the land. This generation of colonial administrators competed for pensions that would support their lifestyle. Beyond pensions, personal and familial glory motivated men like the Vaudreuils. Phillipe de Vaudreuil wanted glory for himself, and he planned for nothing less than his sons to achieve a similar stature within the French empire.

At the ripe age of ten, Pierre de Vaudreuil was given a post within a militia, and by the age of thirteen he had been promoted to the rank of lieutenant—a rank that was purchased within the French empire, not earned by merit nor education. He spent a few years near the court of Versailles under the tutelage of his mother, who was an minorly influential person within imperial circles, and then spent the remainder of his formative years tutored by his father in the business of taming and controlling the Canadian frontier. The elder Vaudreuil died when Pierre was twenty-seven years old, and his mother returned to help the young man manage his family's affairs and secure an appointment for her promising young son. He was given a suitable Canadian appointment in the interim. He was passed over for the governorship of Montreal in 1730, but in 1733 he was given a post as the governor of Trois-Rivières. While Trois-Rivières was small in stature, the position was a full royal governorship. The outpost acted as an important entrance into the Canadian interior and thus provided many opportunities to extract profitable patronage from other settlers.

Dresses like the one displayed here marked the affluence of the society nested within Versailles. Clothing and finery the rest of the empire could not dream about existed in abundance at the empire's center. The younger Vaudreuil's mother ensured that her son never lost his connection to Versailles' affluence and prestige. *Image provided by the Brooklyn Museum Costume Collection at The Metropolitan Museum of Art, Gift of the Brooklyn Museum, 2009; H. Randolph Lever Fund, 1966.*

Pierre de Vaudreuil bided his time as a shrewd gatekeeper in an important Canadian outpost until his matchmaker mother made one last play on her son's behalf. In 1740, Louise-Élisabeth de Joybert, mother of Pierre de Vaudreuil, died in Paris. As fate would have it, when de Vaudreuil arrived in Paris, Bienville's second term as governor was coming to an end. And when the French ministries cast around for a suitable candidate to govern the Louisiana territories, their nets pulled up none other than Pierre de Vaudreuil, son of the great Phillipe de Vaudreuil, who had spent almost a decade perfecting how to manage Trois-Rivières, a frontier province that stood at the foot of a vast colonial interior. The right man for the job secured, Vaudreuil was dispatched to New Orleans in order to manage Louisiana in the name of the king, just as his father had done for Montreal. When Vaudreuil arrived in the New World in 1743, New Orleans lay on the shore, but his eyes were fixed on the distant horizon. He still coveted the position of governor-general of New France. He would have to wade through Louisiana's swamplands to reach his ultimate goal, just as he had done in Trois-Rivières in order to arrive in Louisiana. Ultimately, Vaudreuil would spend ten years knee-deep in the Louisiana muck. By the time he managed to pull himself free of the swamplands in 1753, it was just in time to lose the whole of the empire by the end of the decade.

Vaudreuil's decade as the governor of Louisiana, based out of New Orleans, was spent managing a civil crisis as the colony's money, food and soldiers all seemed moments away from coming undone. The Bad Bread Mutiny discussed in the previous chapter happened during Vaudreuil's term. A year before the mutiny, in 1744, Vaudreuil released a sigh of relief that some bread had arrived by ship in the nick of time. He said, "If flour had not arrived by the S.S. Elephant, the troops would have revolted for account of want of food."[51] The next year, the soldiers in the garrison proved him right—except that they revolted over the quality of the bread Vaudreuil procured for them. For Vaudreuil, the colony needed to be put in working order. Once that was accomplished, it needed to be made more profitable. And ideally, this would also allow for the further exploitation of the continental interior, which would mean even more profit for himself and the empire. Vaudreuil's arrival has been recorded by historians as something of a relief for the upper-class big whites of New Orleans. For them, a Parisian-trained frontier-raised aristocrat with a proven track record and a worldly attitude portended good times. Vaudreuil's arrival was interpreted as a sign that life in the colony might soon get better.

The colony had sunk into an economic recession during the mid-1730s as the colonial currency began to collapse. By 1735, the India Company paper notes that many colonists used as currency were worthless. This collapse led to, in part, the Crown ordering a buyback of India Company money and replacing it with *billets de cartes*. In the wild world of eighteenth-century French currencies, billets de cartes stood for large amounts of livres, which were the official administrative currency of the French kingdom. In theory, livres were backed by a certain amount of French silver, but very few silver livres coins were ever minted by the India Company to address the inflation crisis in its colonies. Once the silver coin livres went into circulation, the paper livres went into permanent decline in the colonies. Why would one accept fanciful paper money when silver coins had their value baked in? Of course, the silver livres never quite lived up to their name. Illinois territory never produced any copper or silver for the empire, so the economic miracle of Spanish silver never occurred in France. The existence of two worthless currencies exacerbated the scarcity crisis in the colony. Only the arrival of Vaudreuil raised the colonists' hopes.

PLAN de la Nlle Orleans
Ville Capitalle de la Louissianne
Explication des Chiffres.
1 Leglise
2 couvent des Capucins
3 la prison
4 corp de garde
5 la place
6 cazernes
7 intendance
8 magazin
9 gouvernement
10 magasin a poudre
11 les jesuistes
12 moulin a vent
13 port des vaisseaux
14 debarquemt. des bateaux
15 la levée
16 baterie de canon
17 fosses
19 isles ou quartiers des habitans
20 proportion d'un isle
22 habitations
23 la briqueterie
24 la fayancerie
25 rüe
26 pont
31 Magazin du Roy
32 lavoir
33 habitation des négres aux jesuites
34 lac
35 canal allant du fleuve au bayou St. jean
36 debarquement des bateaux
ou Fleuve
Missisipy
habitation du Sr. Larche
Des Négres

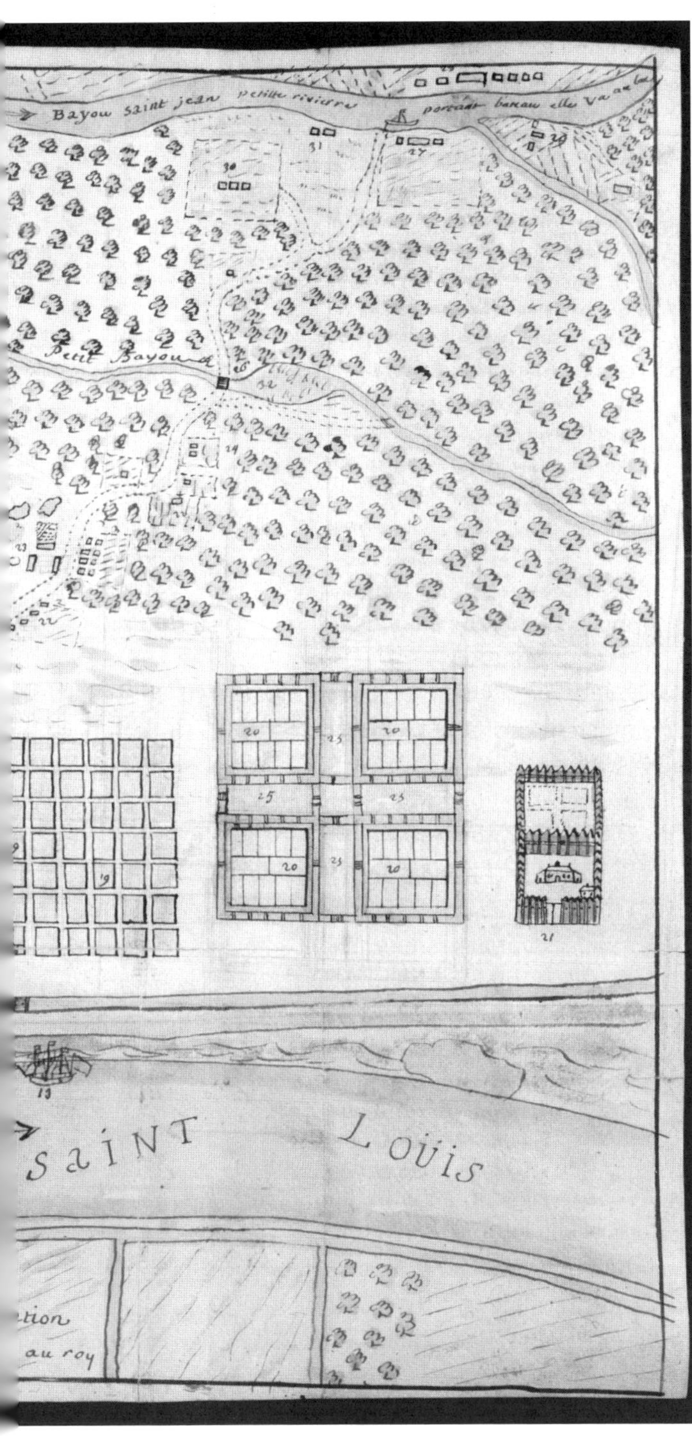

This is a map by Dumont de Montigny that served to re-create the city as it appeared in the 1720s, as a part of his own manuscript published in 1747. *Provided by the Norman B. Leventhal Map & Education Center at the Boston Public Library & the ARGO Collection img9.jpg (11).*

Vaudreuil's reforms attempted to repair some of the damage that decades of administrative mismanagement caused. The big whites being subjects of the Crown, and Governor Vaudreuil being the representative of the Crown in Louisiana, he forced the landowners to build and maintain a system of levies on their properties. If the plantation owners did not comply, Vaudreuil reserved the right to confiscate their land. Although it is unclear if Vaudreuil truly possessed the power to force a confiscation of a major concession, none of the landowners in the colony seemed ready to test the new governor. Vaudreuil's order was obeyed, and this forced them to take basic measures to protect their own crops. It also forced the outlying plantations to maintain a levee system that ultimately benefited New Orleans by protecting it further. Vaudreuil also went to great lengths to ensure that the soldiers were fed their basic rations on a regular schedule. Ultimately, this lowered the quality of the pain de munitions that the soldiers received. But once the Superior Council crushed the dissenters and quieted the rest, Vaudreuil proved capable of putting the bread crisis among the soldiers to rest. He did this by extracting extra wheat and rye from local merchants and small landowners on credit. Sometimes those merchants did not receive prompt payment and had to petition for payment. But Vaudreuil seemed to know which sheep he could shear without causing too much of a ruckus.

Throughout his tenure, Vaudreuil's three economic legacies were his attempts to curtail the currency crisis, his division of the Illinois country's lead mines to a small cartel of French monopolists and tripling the budget of the Louisiana colony between 1742 and 1752. Vaudreuil instituted a popular currency buyback program that alleviated the colonists' money problems. By 1744, the billets de cartes, which essentially acted as bonds for sums of paper livres, had lost so much value that they threatened the colonial economy's stability. Billets de cartes were worth a third of a silver coin livres of the same denomination. Under Vaudreuil's program, the administration bought back the paper money at a ratio of 100 coin livres for every 250 paper livres. This gave the propertied classes a discount and disregarded anyone small enough to have less than 250 paper notes to turn in. The landowners loved this policy, and it put a stable currency into circulation that allowed the other parts of Vaudreuil's economic policies to manifest.

As he appeased the wealthy class and secured a more stable currency for the colony, Vaudreuil decided that the Illinois territory needed to bring in some return on investment for the kingdom. Vaudreuil believed that he had as much of a right to govern the Illinois territory as he had the right to govern New Orleans, and securing prosperity in Illinois and around the Missouri River would allow him to further extend his control into the interior of the country. To this end, Vaudreuil granted a monopoly on the Illinois territory's mines to a Frenchman named Deruisseau. Deruisseau received absolute authority to exploit the region so long as he finished, stocked and populated a fort in the Missouri River area and kept the Native American tribes allied with the French. All of this was done at the expense of the small whites and settlers who slowly began to people the interior of the continent in the mid-eighteenth century. Vaudreuil wanted the few French settlers there to be boxed out of all economic opportunities except farming. In particular, Vaudreuil seems to have been militating against the populations of coureur de bois, trying to strip French settlers of their economic ties with the Native Americans. Those economic ties made the free-roaming frontiersmen impossible to control, while a farmer could be taxed for the state at the royal governor's discretion.

Simple Disagreements of a Colonial Fellow: Rivard du Vigne

For those who decided to settle in Louisiana, they could choose between attempting to establish themselves in or near the colonial towns, like New Orleans, or they could decide to settle a little farther away from the urban centers of the colonial empire. Even before Bienville founded New Orleans, small pockets of French settlers began to carve out places for themselves among the cypress trees and peat swamps. Some of these outlying settlers hardly appear in the historical record. They lived quiet lives away from politics and government, making what money they could from the frontier and surviving from one winter to the next. Richer men who wished to build a fortune claimed swaths of land up and down Louisiana's rivers, forging the patchwork of riverside plantations that resembled the landed noble estates of France. But there was also something like a middle-class settler, a group of people who owned small or medium-sized plots a few miles away from New Orleans. These settlers owned small plots of land and maybe a small number of slaves. They existed between the nameless servants who populated the towns and the wealthy plantation owners and officials who dominated colonial life. This middle class of landed settlers did not invest in the Superior Council's authority because they expected to see a slice of Louisiana's promised profits. Instead, they participated in colonial society because the Superior Council served as the only means to reach a considered legal resolution to the many disputes that appeared in frontier life.

One of the early settlers who falls into this category is Rivard du Vigne. Settlers like Rivard du Vigne, who lived on the edge of the Louisiana wilderness and became the middle class of settlers, first put their roots down in outlying swamplands like Gentilly. Today, Gentilly is a sprawling urban-suburban neighborhood that contains a significant chunk of New Orleans' middle-class families. In the 1720s, all the way through the end of the French colonial era, Gentilly existed as a shifting swamp whose geography centered on Bayou St. John. The bayou provided the all-important throughway between Lake Pontchartrain and the Mississippi River, and men like Rivard du Vigne carefully placed their plots near the bayou so that they could travel across the Isle d'Orleans without much trouble. Positioned within the Gentilly swamplands, settlers like du Vigne could remain apart from the core of colonial society while still participating in the legal and social aspects of colonial life. Settlers like Rivard du Vigne participated in court proceedings, served as witnesses for important documents and spent a good deal of time complaining to the Superior Council about all manner of folly that occurred on the edges of French control. In some ways, this exact ethos still powers Gentilly well into the twenty-first century.

Tracking these settlers can be quite difficult. The names of settlers can vary between notarized documents, while in other cases popular names can appear and reappear across decades. For instance, a Rivard from Gentilly first appeared in May 1723, when Rivard and a collection of other Gentilly settlers filed a petition complaining about stolen cattle.[52] This petition was signed by "A Rivard," who we can assume is the same Antoine Rivard la Vigne that appears in a document from 1725 and the same Rivard du la Vigne that appears across a variety of documents between 1723 and 1728. However, the Rivard who appears in records about ten years later and signed alongside such figures as Attorney General Fleuriau[53] is unlikely to be the same Antoine Rivard de la Vigne but probably the same as Antoine Rivard du Lavigne. French naming conventions and the ways that fathers passed down their names to their sons do not make piecing together the information any easier.[54] And while I cannot assert to have proven definitely one Rivard from another, historians at the Pitot House Museum have done a wonderful job reconstructing life along Bayou St. John in the early eighteenth century. I will use their and other historians' findings as a guide through the life of Rivard dit Lavigne, though we will allow the notarial records to speak within this work.

But, returning to the settlers' complaint, the Natives persisted in stealing cattle. What reason might Native Americans have for stealing cattle in the first place? For the Native Americans in the area, cattle and other Eurasian livestock quickly became some of the most revolutionary imports from Europe to the New World. Native Americans stole these livestock in order to improve their own sources of food. But for the French settlers, those animals were precious as one of the few sources of food that they recognized and trusted. French settlers saw theft of livestock as nothing less than a high crime that needed to be dealt with immediately, far more than a persistent nuisance. The other Gentilly settlers who brought the petition to the Superior Council did not sign the complaint, most likely because only Rivard needed to sign the petition, the other settlers helped present it to the Superior Council, they could not write their own names or some combination of the three. Regardless, the presence of a document complaining about stolen cattle and signed by a Rivard reveals a few things. The document reveals that these settlers could come together to address a common concern. It also reveals that the settlers felt like the Superior Council had a place in policing the frontier or at least the interactions between Natives and settlers.

However, the hardheaded nature of settlers, necessary for remaining steadfast among the heat, humidity and disease of swamplands, also meant that they needed the Superior Council to settle their disputes before they came to blows. In the 1720s, this meant that the Superior Council had to attend to the problems that settlers encountered as European society attempted to transplant itself into North American soil. Unsurprisingly for the swampy muck around Bayou St. John, one of the earliest contentions between settlers in the Gentilly area, at least with regards to the Superior Council, concerned the road system that connected the frontier with New Orleans and beyond. This old road is mentioned in a March 1725 petition submitted to the Superior Council by two settlers who lived in the Gentilly area, along the connection between Lake Pontchartrain and the Mississippi River.[55] The two settlers petitioned the Superior Council because Rivard la Vigne cut off the "original road" that traveled through the Gentilly area and instructed people to begin to use a "new road."[56]

At least two other settlers were having none of it. On March 28, 1725, two Gentilly residents, Lyvet and Soubigne, filed a petition for "Old Right of Way" with the Superior Council in New Orleans. The petition claimed to represent other Gentilly settlers who did not sign, though nothing tells if they had some other way of showing their support. They claimed that Rivard had altered the road so that carts and horses could not pass, and the alternative road could not allow for carts or horses either. Rights of easement, or rights to traverse certain private properties, were an old element of the

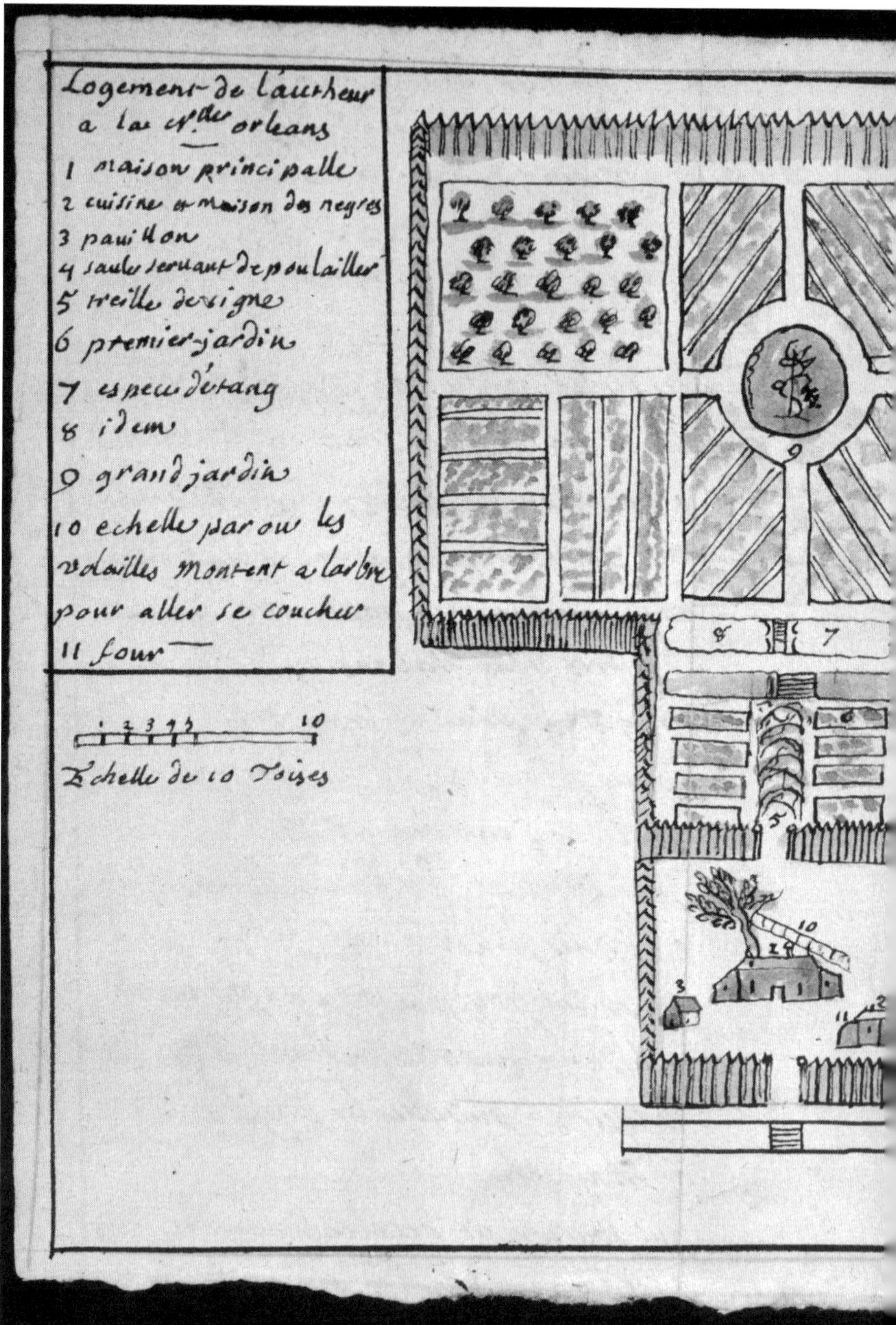
Logement de l'autheur
a la N.lle orleans
1 maison principalle
2 cuisine et maison des negres
3 pauillon
4 saule servant de poulailler
5 treille de vigne
6 premier jardin
7 espece d'etang
8 idem
9 grand jardin
10 echelle par ou les
volailles montent a l'arbre
pour aller se coucher
11 four
1 2 3 4 5 10
Echelle de 10 Toises

This is a drawing by Dumont de Montigny representing what his small homestead looked like in the 1730s. Any sort of colonial breaking and entering would have happened in something bearing a passing resemblance to Monsieur de Montigny's lodgings. *Provided by the Norman B. Leventhal Map & Education Center at the Boston Public Library & the ARGO Collection img10.jpg (12).*

peasant and noble relationship that extended from the middle ages through to modern French law.[57] Ultimately, this precedent was strong enough that the Superior Council decided to order a summons for "Sieur Rivard" that same day. However, at this point, the better part of three months passed before there was any more record on the disagreement. Finally, on June 14, 1725, and after a second petition from the Gentilly settlers for relief, the Superior Council had enough. They summoned Rivard for the next day. On June 21, the council ruled in favor of the settlers. The Superior Council ordered Rivard to either make a suitable new road or restore access to the previous road and bear the costs himself.

If we remember the French legal arguments over slavery and how slavery was allowed to exist in the West Indies but not in France because of the special circumstances of the climate, then the enforcement of the law here becomes doubly interesting and troubling. If the French Superior Council was to be consistent with the opinion of colonial legal scholars, then the moeurs of the new realm should have been allowed to triumph, or at least heard out, by the council. But when a settler presented a persistent problem that threatened carts and horses, getting goods to and from New Orleans and Gentilly, then the old ways were allowed to triumph. It is a ruling over a simple disagreement that reveals the nature of French colonial rule: it was entirely by fiat, with an attitude that never extended beyond "whatever works." The men who participated in the civil process served an important function within the ecosystem of court life. Oftentimes, concessions, successions, wills, official testimonies and petitions needed to be signed by literate witnesses. Anyone who was literate enough to bring forward a petition or a remonstrance was necessarily literate to fulfill these functions. So men like Rivard appear quite a few times in the records as witnesses to various proceedings that went before the Superior Council.

Civil and Uncivil: Lawsuits in Colonial Louisiana

The process of suing another subject of the Crown in Louisiana was not terribly complicated, as long as you could read, write and had learned the various Old World procedures of ancien régime French courts. But if you met those standards, or could pay someone who did, then a lawsuit was only a filed petition away. The petitioner would bring their petition to the Superior Council, which would then decide if the suit had standing within

French law—or if it was worth their time. These petitions held special importance because if they were accepted by the Superior Council and signed as an order, they went into force with the weight of the French courts, and the governor-general's soldiers, behind it. The Superior Council did not sign off on petitioners' wishes without due diligence. At least as often as accepting a petition *prima facie*, they ordered fact finding, summons and further requests for summons. Unless one of the parties had a clear advantage over the other, whether by numbers, Old World precedents or wealth, the Superior Council did spend time going through each step of the legal process. Whether they listened to the facts, the depths of their willingness to see reason or if the decision came before the evidence were other matters entirely. No law or precedent required the Superior Council to provide the reasoning for their rulings, or at least not to include those reasons in the notarized documents.

For a judicial cohort that dealt with a wide range of petty, insolent, cruel and unfortunate cases month after month, they ruled from a place of untouchable authority. The wide range of cases meant that each case was resolved in what amount of paper resembled its value. Particularly for civil cases, the French magistrates often reserved the decisions for a time and then released them in small batches. For instance, on September 12, 1724, the Superior Council in Louisiana released and signed decisions on four cases. Each decision takes up about one-fourth of the piece of paper, though the amount of space given to each is not even. The first case took up nine lines of the page. *Andre Saune v. Defontaine* decided that a man named Defontaine would no longer be the director of a plantation and that Monsieur de Pauger would take his place. After that, the Superior Council decided to put off *Trudeau v. Planchard*, which took up four lines of space. The court resolved *Lasonde v. Coupart* in less than two lines, simply ruling that the plaintiff would not be reimbursed for the cost of the slave he purchased who died soon after as a result of a savage beating. Two lines later, the court spent nine lines resolving a land dispute and dividing the costs and burdens of the disagreement between the litigants of *Delay v. Cabassier*.

Around August 6, 1724, a man with the last name Lasonde bought a Native American girl from an illiterate cabinetmaker in New Orleans named Coupart. She had a slight fever, but Coupart convinced Lasonde that the girl would recover quickly. By August 9, she had not recovered, and around August 10, Lasonde brought "Coupart's slave" to be examined by doctors. The surgeons examined the young woman and came to the same conclusion—her fever resulted from a severe beating that caused significant wounds. The surgeons agreed that she would likely die as a result of the beating and the fever that followed. By the fourteenth, the young woman was likely dead ,as Lasonde filed a petition with the Superior Council over the matter. He felt cheated—Lasonde demanded a refund for the price of the enslaved girl. Coupart protested, saying he had never beaten the girl. Coupart wanted nothing to do with any repayment to Lasonde. The court heard the men out and then a month later released their decision. Lasonde's case was "non-suited," and Lasonde found himself carrying the costs of the case as a penalty. Petty, insolent and unfortunate cases abounded during the colonial era, and the Superior Council served to process them more than bring anything to justice.

Banal cases that revolved around property in one form or another buried the cruelty of cases like Lasonde under a pile of missing cattle, blocked roads, livre notes owed, merchants skipping town and an endless series of concessions and wills to adjudicate. Every criminal act had its reflection in the civil world. For example, on January 27, 1748, around the same time as the Superior Council's trial of Kakaracon over the murder of Pierre Olivy, a small white named Joseph Blanpain received an order to pay the back rent he owed on an enslaved person owned by Jacques Judice. Judice and the council forced Blanpain to pay 550 livres and "costs" of the case. In 1724, around the time that young Marie Lespronne was caught stealing linens, a woman named Jean La Cruse received an order from no less than Bienville to return a pair of shoes to Chaperon and to pay a fine to Chaperon and the city hospital.[58]

Gambling took up the space right on the line between a civil and a criminal infraction. Officially, the royal government in Louisiana disallowed gambling in 1723. Gambling was a moral sin. But more importantly, gambling involved the transfer of property. The Superior Council wanted to control, by reviewing and notarizing, every single transfer of property in the colony. This included intensely personal matters, like the hiring of tutors for children, and purely market concerns like selling and buying any goods. When subjects gambled, they could lose money or property to other subjects without the approval of the Superior Council. In theory, this could make for awkward situations where the winners of a game might rightfully demand a large payment but the loser claimed that the transaction was null without the council's approval. This exact scenario took place in December 1724, when a gentleman named Larche Laine became so drunk while playing cards that he blacked out and woke up to a debt of 4,100 francs.[59] He claimed that since the notes he lost were based on a forbidden game, he should be given time to pay back the debt. The court deliberated for a few days and decided that they would clear the debt and confiscate the notes; Larche would pay 100 livres in fines and a further 300 livres for each time he was caught gambling afterward. The only people the Superior Council wanted to make money was the town hospital, where much of the fine money was sent.

Successions, Conclusions and Concessions

The Superior Council obsessed over concessions and successions. Transfers of land and wealth, especially at the end of a patriarch's life, really defined the bulk of their function. Among the thousands of documents that have been notarized, the vast majority had to do with transfers of wealth between the families of the colonists. The Superior Council's overriding goal was to ensure that this wealth was maintained in a way that explicitly benefited the kingdom, the people on the Superior Council and the other powerful members of New Orleans society. Attempting to trace the transfers of land and resources, slaves and wives, tutors and children as if they were some grand conspiracy is too large a task. Beyond genealogical purposes, cataloguing the thousands of notarized transfers that occurred in the French period could serve no purpose. It might provide one with a high-definition view of the shifting control of territory in New France, but that is data without an argument. As a whole, I have submitted to the crushing weight of the civil record within French Louisiana. No more litigious people may have ever existed on a frontier. For a group of people who made their living as far away from Versailles and the king as possible, they certainly demanded the king's presence whenever the slightest quarrel over property arose. The civil record demands more to interpret as well. In cases of criminal trial, the Superior Council often looked for information in ways that make their actions and intentions obvious. Civil cases, marriages, deaths, the movement of money and land, all of this is more nuanced and requires a far finer comb through the present records. All to discover that French settlers bickered over basic supplies and sums of livres totaling between twenty and fifteen thousand.

The burning question becomes *why* did the French take such detailed recordings of every livres and acre? It feels like the accumulation of papers served some other purpose. Taking a step back and looking at the genre of document broadly, a few details step out and seem useful. By cataloguing every transfer of wealth that they could, the Superior Council could keep a strong sense of exactly how much wealth was in the colony and how much was making its way back to France. Vaudreuil used his good rapport with the Superior Council and position as governor to do exactly that—his good accounting being a good indication of his legacy as the colony's financial godfather. Capping off Vaudreuil's pro-wealth regime, he was at least partially responsible for the trade of the colony nearly doubling in the 1750s and the money being spent on the colony tripling over a ten-year period. How Vaudreuil accomplished these most astounding feats is also the most frustratingly obscure part of his tenure. In the same span, Vaudreuil continued Bienville's practice of tolerating trade with Spanish and English smugglers. It could be that Vaudreuil recognized that the Port of Orleans needed to be freed, but that probably ascribes too much intent on his part. He certainly was no early champion of free markets. Smuggling made basic and luxury goods cheaper. In turn, more goods and lower prices kept the wealthy and the middle classes happy and allowed everyone to spend more paper money to stimulate the failing French economy. Governors who were popular intuited or copied this policy of lax port enforcement. The governors who kept a fastidious track of shipping taxes tended to be the least popular with the people of the colony.

In the final review, the Superior Council held more important wells of power than the governors of Louisiana ever did. This can be frustrating

Depictions of vigorous trade between European settlers and Native Americans are relatively uncommon. Here, an artist in 1717 depicts his vision of trade between New France and the Native Americans within those borders. *Retrieved from the Library of Congress Digital Collection img2.png.*

because the men of the Superior Council are harder to track through the historical record than the succession of singular governors that stretches from Bienville to Charles Philip Aubry, the last royal governor of Louisiana. The members of the Superior Council were landowners and colonists with an investment in the colony and the trusted appointment of the ministers from Versailles. They had endless practice with oratory and negotiation. As time went on, a greater population of native-born Creoles took charge of the local governmental affairs. Their soft power as a class grew as well. Their power and influence within the Basse-Louisiane reached its zenith with the arrival of German and Acadian settlers in the region. By the 1760s, a distinct population of native residents had developed to the point where their interests diverged from those of the French empire. The result was the catastrophic uprising in 1768 against Spanish rule.

The final straw on the path to revolt was Governor Ulloa's resistance to working with the Superior Council at all. Channeling a bit of the ancien régime way of doing things, Ulloa used Aubry to go around the Superior Council. He did not ask the council for its advice, and he never presented his reform programs to the Superior Council. Ulloa was as loyal to the Spanish empire as Aubry was to the French empire, and neither held a particular loyalty to the territory of Louisiana or its people. When the Creole elite rose up in 1768 against the Spanish governor, a wealthy and charismatic scion of the planter class, Lafreniere, became the spokesman of the colonists' short-lived revolution. The Superior Council positioned itself from the beginning of the 1768 revolt to become the acting government of the colony, and Lafreniere, along with his conspirator Foucault, folded nicely into that reality. When Aubry grew suspicious of the brewing revolt, Lafreniere calmed the interim governor and convinced him that the colonists meant no harm to the Spanish governor or the Spanish colonists beginning to settle in the area. When Aubry finally had enough, or was forced to confront the reality of the insurrection against the Spanish Crown, he petitioned the Superior Council to put an end to the sedition. When madness descended on the colonists and Lafreniere's men decided that the Spanish warship parked in the harbor had to be repelled by force, Aubry put himself in front of a colonial militia led by Creole planters and told them that he would die before they harmed the Spanish warship or the people aboard. The Superior Council and the Creole planters that controlled it were the first, and only, colonial institution to side with the territory of Louisiana over a foreign power.

For a few months in 1768, the Creole colonists could see their ideal manifest against the reality of Louisiana's environment. Aubry tried to warn them of their folly, but it was too late. Whether they vocalized a desire for independence, or whether they believed it was possible, the result was the same. For a few months, the Louisiana territory was independent. During that time, every intrinsic problem of the colony was laid bare. The few months that Louisiana had to go without explicit support from a European empire resulted in a loss of cash, a loss of goods and the basic supplies for everyday life drying up. While contemporaries assigned the failure of the revolution to a number of factors, including a racist preoccupation with the abilities of the colonists to launch a revolution, Governor Aubry, in his second address to the Superior Council over the course of the revolt came closest to the truth. He warned them that Louisiana could not be independent. It lacked the resources to sustain itself. The territory had never produced enough to feed itself, house itself and provide for its inhabitants' needs. He warned that without the Spanish treasurer residing within the colony, there would be no currency with which to do business. The ideals of the insurrectionaries could not survive in the environment they wanted to cultivate. It seemed as if launching an Enlightenment-style revolution in Louisiana was like trying to plant a seed in the wrong soil.

Still, these events presaged the French and American revolutions. And still others like Anne Mony had foreshadowed the revolt of 1768. Anne Mony's drive for freedom from the tyranny of France, as a baker's wife, almost certainly had to do with economic freedom—the freedom to buy and sell outside of the empire's own stock. The dazzling myriad of disputes over currency, land, commodities, paper notes and slaves over the preceding forty years had not been a series of isolated incidents that simply confirmed that bad apples spoil the basket. Instead, every civil suit, every concession, every contested succession, every charge of smuggling and fleeing taxes and stealing cargo, every monopoly given and every slave and miner imported into the colony all served to prop up the fundamental reality that the Superior Council refused to recognize. The Louisiana territory could not, and never would be, independent and wealthy of its own accord. From its inception, Louisiana was a dependency of a greater empire. No amount of power secured over the colony, nor any heavy-handed ruling by legislative fiat, would change that simple fact. The Louisiana territory that the Creole elite and imperial administrators had created together over four decades could never be separate from the empire because it was a deeply unequal and dependent society.

REFLECTIONS

I tell my students that history is messy. A good line of historical inquiry will have no clear answer. Unless the question solves itself, unless the investigation is so narrow as to become self-referential, history does not present us with clear narratives that answer discrete questions. Instead, historians live among the avalanche of primary source data, secondary source investigations, archaeological findings, folklore, gossip and gut feelings. Stuck in a bleak landfill of centuries-old refuse, historians string together facts so that they can fly like kites in the wind, go this way and that, and bring a little meaning to the current day. There are certainly monumental works of history, works like Gibbon's *Rise and Fall of the Roman Empire*, that attempt to find inalienable facts every step of the way. These are the titanic historians of our era. Their works are monuments to the art of building history. Histories of the small, like the book you hold in your hands now, rely on the hard work done by the gigantic, complex, broad history books. In turn, historians of the small hope that these works will build toward another gifted historian's magnum opus. With this work, I aimed to give color to the histories that many of us know. Any good history teacher knows that *colorful* histories are *remembered* histories. I was lucky that this topic had so many colorful characters and events along the way.

New Orleans, French Louisiana, New France—by whatever name—is a messy subject in a messy field. In the current day, even the boundaries of New Orleans as a cultural construct are beginning to blur. The mass of urban, suburban, commercial and industrial development carries official names like Kenner, Metairie, St. Rose, Westwego, but someone from any of those places could not be blamed for saying they are "from New Orleans." The Greater New Orleans area has become a single economic, social and political unit that functions as a single culture. From the perspective of the twenty-first century, when the city spans the entire land mass between the Mississippi River and Lake Pontchartrain, New Orleans refuses to yield even a clear founding date. European settlement in the Orleans Parish area started as early as 1709 with the wave of settlers to Gentilly that brought folk like Rivard du Vigne into the colony. Bienville did not found New Orleans until nine years later. The French empire left the colony's administration in tangles. Administrators never got along, formed factions aimed at one another and left few records of their individual misdeeds. Meanwhile, men and women press-ganged into awful conditions suddenly found themselves up against unprecedented desperation. They did not leave a wealth of diaries and personal artifacts that provide individual insight into their lives. Instead, they left behind impressions where their lives bounced against the imperial administrators—the only people writing anything down with any regularity. None of them were particularly interested in the "founding date" of the world they found themselves in. The history of New Orleans is nebulous, murky like bayou water.

Fittingly for New Orleans, this is a book of ghost stories. Marie Lespronne, Anne Mony, Vaudreuil, Kakaracon, this book is the collected impressions of their lives left behind in old notary stacks. Certainly none of them wanted to be remembered through old court records. A woman like Anne Mony wanted freedom as much as an enslaved African like Kakaracon. Marie Lespronne most likely wanted simple daily comforts. Vaudreuil wanted glory and prestige within the French empire. They all had dreams that are completely lost to the historical record. All that has been left are what others recorded about them in their worst moments. I have attempted to take these moments and weave them into stories. These stories strive to catch some of the color of their lives. But most importantly, this book seeks to make the reasons for their choices, the reasons that they lived in horrid conditions at the edge of the known world, rational and sensible. This is more than a crusade to write interesting and important, if lesser, characters into the historical record—I hope the reader feels that this book illuminates *why* people thought and acted the way they did in colonial Louisiana.

I tell my students that history is a dark forest. In order to navigate a dark forest, people need guideposts. Otherwise, they will get lost and never make it to their destination. This book was made to serve as a set of guideposts for understanding the dark, twisting pathways of New France. It is hard to visualize the lifestyle of a young woman in the French Quarter circa 1724 when your only experience is walking down Decatur Street during the height of tourist season. While anyone who walks New Orleans' streets has physical access to the location of deep history, just that access does not bring anyone closer to understanding how the world was—or why our world is the way it is. But it is my hope that after you read about Marie Lespronne and Diderot, about Bon Temps and Guillory, walking through New Orleans becomes a more enlightened experience. The mud under New Orleans is too thick and the past sinks too quickly for this book to ever be a literal tour guide. The buildings from the French era would have been largely destroyed by fires and hurricanes during the Spanish era. Much of the archaeological evidence for colonization is trapped beneath the French Quarter's cobblestone. But knowing the pressures of colonial life, knowing what people stole, why they ran from their masters and what fates awaited those condemned to die gives us a meter to judge our own experiences in Louisiana against. Traversing the Greater New Orleans area with these histories in mind colors the experience in an entirely new way.

The book rests on the premise that three major factors contributed to the rate and character of crime in colonial Louisiana. First, the subtropical climate and acute weather conditions pushed the temperate-inclined Europeans to the edge. This argument does not imply that the Europeans could not handle the heat. Rather, their supplies, their crops, the way they provisioned their food and maintained their ships all suffered under weather patterns they were unprepared for. Second, the expansiveness of the Louisiana territory meant that the French empire could never hope to fully control the full expanse of the land and exploit it. Exploiting the vast interior of the continent was an impossible task. Men at all levels of French society talked up the possibility of silver hidden deep within Illinois country. These tales only covered up the greater truth—only silver on the scale the Spanish found in Mexico could ever hope to draw the money, people and resources needed to control the entire Mississippi River basin. Merchant schemes, tall tales, unfettered coureurs de bois, wild dealings with the Native Americans, illegal trading with the English and isolated garrisons filled the vacuum. Third, the colonial system was destined for failure. The fatal mix of speculative capitalism with strong mercantilist policies left the people starved for cash, resources and opportunities to gather either of those. The upper class became permanently embattled as they struggled to maintain their luxurious lifestyles and the profitability of their plantations. Crime grew from desperation without any source of relief.

These principles serve as a fair set of guideposts for almost any point in Louisiana's history. None of this is groundbreaking research. Much of the research in this book is limited to the Gulf Coast and the New Orleans area. Instead, looking at the sum total of our knowledge of crime in colonial Louisiana, we can draw out these few general principles and use them to navigate the dark forest of history. There is far more to Louisiana history than the borders of the modern state of Louisiana. A firm understanding of Louisiana's colonial history enlightens the history of places as far away as St. Louis and Detroit. I hope the lessons within this book are compelling enough that they cause you to ask questions about how the environment, government and geography of our country affect the world around us today. It is not enough to analyze how the environment in Louisiana drove the colonists to the edge of desperation and beyond. We should carefully pay attention to how the current environment of Louisiana is pushing people beyond the point of desperation—and how the causes have not changed very much over the last two hundred years.

Louisiana needs brave historians. In the final estimation of a survey of crime in colonial Louisiana, many of these stories should have been shared long before now. Compelling, interesting human stories have been left in archives partially because histories of Louisiana, and especially histories of New Orleans, need to conform to a particular, tourist-friendly view of the city. Bayous, alligators, fishing, Mardi Gras, cobblestone streets, levees and jazz music are all acceptable topics for Louisiana history. These topics drive tourism, and they also bolster a sense of community and culture. There is nothing wrong with this. Tourism employs a huge portion of the Greater New Orleans region. Jazz, bayous and gumbo are legitimate parts of our culture and legitimate subjects of study. But our relationship with crime, imperialism, larceny, slavery, exploitation and murder goes unexplored because we often lack the bravery to face the darker aspects of our history. This does not mean that these dark moments in history have no effect on us. Quite the opposite—by choosing ignorance, we allow the past to do whatever it wants with us. By ignoring the history of the Code Noir and the effect it had on postcolonial Louisiana, we allow the Code Noir's influence to rampage unmitigated across our communities. Historians are the first and last line of defense against history having its way with us.

NOTES

Introduction

1. Brasseaux, "Moral Climate of French Colonial Louisiana," 30.
2. Brasseaux, "Moral Climate of French Colonial Louisiana, 27–41."
3 . Spear, "Colonial Intimacies," 75–98.
4. Gould, "Bienville's Brides," 389–408; Robenstine, "French Colonial Policy," 193–211; DuVal, "Indian Intermarriage and Métissage," 267–304.
5. Barr, "From Captives to Slaves," 19–46.
6 . Brasseaux, "Moral Climate of French Colonial Louisiana, 32.'
7. Cusick, "Slanders and Sodomy," 415–18.
8. Brasseaux, "Moral Climate of French Colonial Louisiana," 27–41.
9. Cusick, "Slanders and Sodomy," 415–45.
10. Usner, "American Indians in Colonial New Orleans," 163–86.
11. Sayre, "Plotting the Natchez Massacre," 381–413.
12. Nicole Jean-Louis, *Branded With Fleur De Lis A Symbolic Link To Slavery*, https://fineartamerica.com.

Chapter 1

13. August 2, 1717. "1852.13 2 Aug. 1717. Royal Declaration for the Preservation of All Drafts Made by Notaries."
14. de Lambilly, "Garlic, Hot Chocolate."
15. Baker, "'Cherchez Les Femmes,'" 21–37.
16. "Criminal Procedure: Investigation of nocturnal robbery. Examination of witnesses," #1723-05-22-01. Hereafter, all period legal documents will be identified by short titles and Date/ID numbers. A searchable timeline of these

and related documents may be found at the Louisiana Historical Center's Louisiana Colonial Documents Digitization Projects site: https://www.lacolonialdocs.org/search.

17. "Criminal Proceedings," #1723-07-13-01.
18. "Criminal Proceedings," #1723-07-15-01.
19. Spear, "Colonial Intimacies," 90–93.
20. National Weather Service, "New Orleans/Baton Rouge New 30 Year Climate Normals."
21. "Marine Abduction Plot Interrogatory: Marin Lafontaine," #1723-07-29-02.
22. Surrey and Waselkov, *Commerce of Louisiana.*
23. "Marine Abduction Plot Interrogatory: Pierre Chauvin," #1723-08-17-01.
24. "Marine Abduction Plot Interrogatory: Francois Millat," #1723-09-22-02.
25. "Marine Abduction Plot. Testimony on Desertion Plot." #1723-09-24-02.
26. "Marine Abduction Plot Confronting Process," #1723-09-25-04.
27. "Marine Abduction Plot. Petition for Legal Counsel," #1723-10-10-01.
28. Fourastié, "Wages and Purchasing Power."
29. "Criminal Suit. The Procurator General vs. Laborde," #1722-11-17-01.

Chapter 2

30. Chatman, "'There Are No Slaves in France,'" 144–53.
31. Ghachem, "Montesquieu in the Caribbean," 183–210.
32. Garrigus, "'Code Noir' (1685)."
33. Palmer, "Code Noir of 1724."
34. Garrigus, "'Code Noir' (1685)."
35. Palmer, "Code Noir of 1724."
36. "Examination of Bontemps and Guillory," #1728-06-14-03.
37. "Examination of Bontemps and Guillory," #1728-06-05-01.
38. "Examination of Bontemps and Guillory," #1728-06-05-02.
39. "Document No. D413," #1741-01-10-01.
40. "Prosecution and Examination of runaway slave named Pierrot," #1741-01-16-01.
41. "Prosecution and examination of runaway slaves," #1741-01-16-03.
42. "Petition to Recover Runaway Slave," 1730-11-13-02.
43. Pasquier, "Louisiana's Code Noir (1724)."
44. "Remonstrance made by D'Auseville," #1739-12-14-05.
45. "Condemnation of Kakaracon," 1748-01-10-02.
46. Palmer, "Code Noir of 1724."
47. Law Library of Louisiana, "History of the Codes of Louisiana."
48. National Park Service, "U.S. Takes Possession of Louisiana."

Chapter 3

49. "Civil Suit," #1724-02-09-02.
50. "Report of De Lisle Dupart," #1747-03-10-03.
51. Gayarré, *History of Louisiana*, Lecture 1.
52. "Complaint of Rivard and others of theft," #1723-05-24-02.
53. "Succession of Dame Marie Anne Bertin, Widow," #1739-11-28-01.
54. FamilySearch. "Antoine François Rivard dit Lavigne."
55. "Petition for old right of way," #1725-03-28-01, March 28, 1725.
56. "Petition for old right of way."
57. O'Connor, "Can I Challenge a Historic Right of Way"; Vern, "Land Registration Systems & Discourses of Property," 835–52; Munford, "Conscription and the Peasants," 1–18.
58. "French Translations, July 1724–December 1724," page 11, no. 60.
59. *Louisiana Historical Quarterly*, vol. 1.

BIBLIOGRAPHY

Secondary Sources

Baker, Vaughan B. "'Cherchez Les Femmes': Some Glimpses of Women in Early Eighteenth-Century Louisiana." *Louisiana History: The Journal of the Louisiana Historical Association* 31, no. 1 (1990): 21–37.

Barr, Juliana. "From Captives to Slaves: Commodifying Indian Women in the Borderlands." *Journal of American History* 92, no. 1 (2005): 19–46.

Brasseaux, Carl A. "The Moral Climate of French Colonial Louisiana, 1699–1763." *Louisiana History: The Journal of the Louisiana Historical Association* 27, no. 1 (1986): 27–41.

Brown, Mark. "Colonial States, Colonial Rule, Colonial Governmentalities: Implications for the Study of Historical State Crime." *State Crime Journal* 7, no. 2 (2018): 173–98.

Chatman, Samuel L. "'There Are No Slaves in France': A Re-Examination of Slave Laws in Eighteenth Century France." *Journal of Negro History* 85, no. 3 (2000): 144–53.

Coutts, Brian E. "Etienne De Périer." 64 Parishes. October 14, 2024. https://64parishes.org.

Cowan, Walter Greaves, and Jack B. McGuire. *Louisiana Governors: Rulers, Rascals, and Reformers*. University Press of Mississippi, 2008.

Cusick, James G. "Slanders and Sodomy: Studying the Past Through Colonial Crime Investigation." *Florida Historical Quarterly* 93, no. 3 (2015): 415–45.

de Lambilly, Joséphine. "Garlic, Hot Chocolate: These Were the Favorite Dishes of the Kinds of France." *En-Vols*, June 2023. https://www.en-vols.com.

Dictionary of Canadian Biography. "Le Moyne de Bienville, Jean-Baptiste." Dictionary of Canadian Biography. https://www.biographi.ca.

DuVal, Kathleen. "Indian Intermarriage and Métissage in Colonial Louisiana." *William and Mary Quarterly* 65, no. 2 (2008): 267–304.

FamilySearch. "Antoine François Rivard dit Lavigne." https://ancestors.familysearch.org.

Fourastié, Jean. "Wages and Purchasing Power in France." https://www.fourastie-sauvy.org.

Gayarré, Charles. *History of Louisiana.* 1st ed. William J. Windleton, 1867. https://penelope.uchicago.edu/Thayer/E/Gazetteer/Places/America/United_States/Louisiana/_Texts/GAYHLA/home.html

Ghachem, Malick W. "Montesquieu in the Caribbean: The Colonial Enlightenment between 'Code Noir' and 'Code Civil.'" *Historical Reflections / Réflexions Historiques* 25, no. 2 (1999): 183–210.

Gould, Virginia. "Bienville's Brides: Virgins or Prostitutes? 1719–1721." *Louisiana History: The Journal of the Louisiana Historical Association* 59, no. 4 (2018): 389–408.

Kehoe, Thomas J., Jeffrey Pfeifer and Jason Skues. "From Prison to Society: Characterising Crime in Colonial Australia Using the Records of the Court of Criminal Jurisdiction." *Crime, Histoire & Sociétés / Crime, History & Societies* 23, no. 1 (2019): 47–64.

Law Library of Louisiana. "History of the Codes of Louisiana: Black Code." https://lasc.libguides.com.

Library of Congress. "Louisiana as a French Colony | Articles and Essays | Louisiana: European Explorations and the Louisiana Purchase | Digital Collections | Library of Congress," n.d. https://www.loc.gov.

Louisiana Historical Quarterly, vol. 1. Louisiana Historical Society, 1917. 1st ed. Digitized. https://babel.hathitrust.org.

Moen, Jon. "John Law and the Mississippi Bubble: 1718–1720." Mississippi History Now, October 2001. https://www.mshistorynow.mdah.ms.gov.

Moogk, Peter. "Manon Lescaut's Countrymen: Emigration from France to North America Before 1763." *Proceedings of the Meeting of the French Colonial Historical Society* 16 (1992): 24–44.

Munford, Clarence J. "Conscription and the Peasants of the Morvan District of Chateau-Chinon, 1792–1794." *Journal of History* 4, no. 2 (September 1, 1969): 1–18.

National Park Service. "U.S. Takes Possession of Louisiana." https://www.nps.gov.

National Weather Service. "New Orleans/Baton Rouge New 30 Year Climate Normals (1991–2020)." https://www.weather.gov.

O'Connor, Sean. "Can I Challenge a Historic Right of Way Over My Private French Property—Complete France." Complete France, April 8, 2022. https://www.completefrance.com.

Pasquier, Michael T. "Code Noir." 64 Parishes. February 26, 2024. https://64parishes.org/entry/code-noir-adaptation.

Robenstine, Clark. "French Colonial Policy and the Education of Women and Minorities: Louisiana in the Early Eighteenth Century." *History of Education Quarterly* 32, no. 2 (1992): 193–211.

Sayre, Gordon. "Plotting the Natchez Massacre: Le Page Du Pratz, Dumont de Montigny, Chateaubriand." *Early American Literature* 37, no. 3 (2002): 381–413.

Spear, Jennifer M. "Colonial Intimacies: Legislating Sex in French Louisiana." *William and Mary Quarterly* 60, no. 1 (2003): 75–98.

Surrey, Nancy Maria Miller, and Gregory A. Waselkov. *The Commerce of Louisiana During the French Regime: 1699–1763*. University of Alabama Press, 2006.

Undiscovered Scotland. "John Law." © Undiscovered Scotland. https://www.undiscoveredscotland.co.uk.

University of South Alabama. "Meet the Colonists | Center for Archaeological Studies." https://www.southalabama.edu.

Usner, Daniel H. "American Indians in Colonial New Orleans." In *Powhatan's Mantle: Indians in the Colonial Southeast, Revised and Expanded Edition*, edited by Gregory A. Waselkov, Peter H. Wood, and Tom Hatley, 163–86. University of Nebraska Press, 2006.

Vern, Flora. "Land Registration Systems & Discourses of Property." *European Review of Private Law* 29, no. 6 (2021): 835–52.

Primary Sources

"Carte de la coste du nouveau Biloxy avec les isles des environs pour faire voir la situation de la rade de l'isle aux vaisseaux, et celle de l'isle de la Chandeleur." 18th century map. Scale. https://gallica.bnf.fr/ark:/12148/btv1b8596069n/f1.item.zoom#.

Centenary College of Louisiana. "Le Code Noir de La Louisiane—1724." http://french.centenary.edu/codenoir.htm.

"Civil Suit: Adrien de Pauger vs. Bienville." #1724-02-09-02. February 9, 1724. Louisiana Historical Center, Louisiana Colonial Documents Digitization project [hereafter LCDD]. https://www.lacolonialdocs.org/document/130.

"Complaint of Rivard and others of theft of cattle by savages." #1723-05-24-02. May 24, 1723. Louisiana Historical Center, LCDD. https://www.lacolonialdocs.org/document/50.

"Condemnation of Kakaracon." #1748-01-10-02. January 10, 1748. Louisiana Historical Center, LCDD. https://www.lacolonialdocs.org/document/7828.

"Criminal Procedure: Investigation of nocturnal robbery." #1723-05-22-01. May 22, 1723. Louisiana Historical Center, LCDD. https://www.lacolonialdocs.org/document/46.

"Criminal Procedure: Investigation of nocturnal robbery. Examination of witnesses." #1723-05-25-01. May 25, 1723. Louisiana Historical Center, LCDD. https://www.lacolonialdocs.org/document/51.

"Criminal Proceedings: Joseph Chapron vs. LeRoy and wife." #1723-07-13-01. July 13, 1723. Louisiana Historical Center, LCDD. https://www.lacolonialdocs.org/document/59.

"Criminal Proceedings: Joseph Chapron vs. LeRoy and wife." #1723-07-14-01. July 14, 1723. Louisiana Historical Center, LCDD. https://www.lacolonialdocs.org/document/60.

"Criminal Proceedings: Joseph Chapron vs. LeRoy and wife." #1723-07-15-01. July 15, 1723. Louisiana Historical Center, LCDD. https://www.lacolonialdocs.org/document/62.

"Criminal Suit. The Procurator General vs. Laborde." #1722-11-17-01. November 17, 1722. Manuscript. Louisiana Historical Center, LCDD. https://www.lacolonialdocs.org/document/35.

"Document No. D413." #1741-01-10-01. January 1, 1741. Louisiana Historical Center, LCDD. https://www.lacolonialdocs.org/document/5134.

"1852.13 2 Aug. 1717. Royal Declaration for the Preservation of All Drafts Made by Notaries." French Manuscripts, Mississippi Valley, 1679–1769. Louisiana Office of the Lieutenant Governor, Department of Culture Recreation & Tourism. https://www.crt.state.la.us.

"Examination of Bontemps and Guillory Savage Slaves of Srs. Pellerin and Trudeau Document 28/74." #1728-06-05-01. June 5, 1728. Louisiana Historical Center, LCDD. https://www.lacolonialdocs.org/document/1321.

"Examination of Bontemps and Guillory Savage Slaves of Srs. Pellerin and Trudeau. Document 28/75." #1728-06-05-02. June 5, 1728. Louisiana Historical Center, LCDD. https://www.lacolonialdocs.org/document/1322.

"Examination of Bontemps and Guillory Savage Slaves of Srs. Pellerin and Trudeau Document 28/77." #1728-06-14-03. June 14, 1728. Louisiana Historical Center, LCDD. https://www.lacolonialdocs.org/document/1330.

"French Translations, July 1724–December 1724." French Manuscripts, Mississippi Valley, 1679–1769. Louisiana Office of the Lieutenant Governor, Department of Culture Recreation & Tourism. https://www.crt.state.la.us.

Garrigus, John, trans. "The 'Code Noir' (1685)." Washington State University. https://s3.wp.wsu.edu/uploads/sites/1205/2016/02/code-noir.pdf.

"Marine Abduction Plot Confronting Process." #1723-09-25-04. September 25, 1723. Louisiana Historical Center, LCDD. https://www.lacolonialdocs.org/document/377.

"Marine Abduction Plot Interrogatory: Francois Millat." #1723-09-22-02. September 22, 1723. Louisiana Historical Center, LCDD. https://www.lacolonialdocs.org/document/73.

"Marine Abduction Plot Interrogatory: Marin Lafontaine." #1723-07-29-02. July 29, 1723. Louisiana Historical Center, LCDD. https://www.lacolonialdocs.org/document/64.

"Marine Abduction Plot Interrogatory: Pierre Chauvin." #1723-08-17-01. August 17, 1723. Louisiana Historical Center, LCDD. https://www.lacolonialdocs.org/document/68.

"Marine Abduction Plot. Petition for Legal Counsel." #1723-10-10-01. October 10, 1723. Louisiana Historical Center, LCDD. https://www.lacolonialdocs.org/document/91.

"Marine Abduction Plot. Testimony on Desertion Plot." #1723-09-24-02. September 24, 1723. Louisiana Historical Society, LCDD. https://www.lacolonialdocs.org/document/77.

Palmer, Vernon Valentine, trans. "The Code Noir of 1724." *Tulane European & Civil Law Forum* 34 (2019): 104–129. https://journals.tulane.edu/teclf/article/view/2887/2707.

"Petition for old right of way." #1725-03-28-01. March 28, 1725. Louisiana Historical Society, LCDD. https://www.lacolonialdocs.org/document/377.

"Petition to Recover Runaway Slave." #1730-11-13-02. November 13, 1730. Louisiana Historical Society, LCDD. https://www.lacolonialdocs.org/document/1949.

"Prosecution and examination of runaway slave named Pierrot." #1741-01-16-03. January 16, 1741. Louisiana Historical Center, LCDD. https://www.lacolonialdocs.org/document/5145.

"Prosecution and examination of runaway slaves." #1741-01-16-01. January 16, 1741. Louisiana Historical Center, LCDD. https://www.lacolonialdocs.org/document/5143.

"Remonstrance made by D'Auseville realtive [*sic*] to the murder of his negro slave." #1739-12-14-05. December 14, 1739. Louisiana Historical Center, LCDD. https://www.lacolonialdocs.org/document/4664.

"Report of De Lisle Dupart of a rumor in Havana that a boat crew commanded by Capt. Auvray had carried away black slaves from New Orleans." #1747-03-10-03. March 10, 1747. Louisiana Historical Center, LCDD. https://www.lacolonialdocs.org/document/7379.

"Succession of Dame Marie Anne Bertin, Widow." #1739-11-28-01. November 28, 1739. Louisiana Historical Center, LCDD. https://www.lacolonialdocs.org/document/4630.

ABOUT THE AUTHOR

David Michael Schneider is a high school educator in New Orleans, Louisiana. He grew up in the Greater New Orleans area and has spent his life submerged in Louisiana's unique culture. He received his bachelor's in philosophy of religious studies from Louisiana State University and also received a minor in political science. He practices historic forms of European swordplay with the Crescent City Historical Fencing Club and continues to work within New Orleans to discover important local histories.